Lives in Cricket: No

Edgar Willsher
The Lion of Kent

Giles Phillips

With a foreword by Derek Underwood

First published in Great Britain by
Association of Cricket Statisticians and Historians
Cardiff CF11 9XR.
© ACS, 2012

Giles Phillips has asserted his right under the Copyright, Designs
and Patents Act 1988 to be identified as the author of this work.

All Rights Reserved. No part of this publication may be reproduced, stored in a
retrieval system, or transmitted in any form, or by any means, electronic,
mechanical, photocopying, recording or otherwise without the prior permission in
writing of the Copyright holders, nor be otherwise circulated in any form, or
binding or cover other than in which it is published and without a similar condition
including this condition being imposed on the subsequent publisher.

British Library Cataloguing-in-Publication Data.
A catalogue record for this book is available from the British Library.

ISBN: 978 1 908165 15 2
Typeset and printed by The City Press Leeds Ltd

Contents

Foreword		5
Chapter One	Origins	7
Chapter Two	Moving On	12
Chapter Three	The Big Time	15
Chapter Four	Methods	18
Chapter Five	With the All-England Eleven	24
Chapter Six	At Enville Hall	27
Chapter Seven	Willsher's Hand is Very High	34
Chapter Eight	Incident at The Oval	39
Chapter Nine	Overarm at Last	45
Chapter Ten	Captain of England	53
Chapter Eleven	Cricket on the Brain	69
Chapter Twelve	Winding Down	84
Chapter Thirteen	Epitaph	92
Acknowledgements		99
Bibliography		100
Appendix	Career Statistics	102
Index		106

Foreword
by Derek Underwood, MBE

When I began my Kent career as a 17-year-old in 1963, I was fortunate enough to be captained by my boyhood hero, Colin Cowdrey. Already we were a promising side and as the 1960s wore on we developed into an outstanding one. England internationals such as Brian Luckhurst, Mike Denness, Alan Knott and Bob Woolmer were joined by overseas allrounders like John Shepherd, Asif Iqbal and Bernard Julien to form the dominant county squad of the 1970s. It was a golden era for Kent cricket, and I am proud to have played a part in it.

Since my retirement, the county's fortunes have been in decline, but there is no reason why it cannot be successful again in the future. I was struck by this thought when reading the story of Edgar Willsher, a fellow left-arm bowler from a much earlier era. Unlike me he played in a poor Kent side, and had to bear the brunt of the attack with little support for a quarter of a century, from 1850 to 1875. But he just missed out on forming part of the all-conquering sides of the 1830s and 1840s, whose great names included the legendary Fuller Pilch and Alfred Mynn. What an attack it would have been if Willsher had been born a decade or so earlier!

From the account given in Giles Phillips' biography, it seems clear that Willsher was one of our greatest-ever bowlers and on that count alone this book deserves a wide audience. But there is a lot more to the story than that. Just as I played at a time of great upheaval with the introduction of the one-day game into county cricket, so he saw huge changes during his lifetime, including the transition from round-arm to over-arm bowling, and the beginning of overseas tours. All this makes me feel a much closer connection to Willsher and the cricketers of his time, and gives me hope that great players like him will emerge in time so that Kentish cricket can thrive once again.

Paddock Wood, Kent
January 2012

Chapter One
Origins

This ROLVENDEN is a very beautiful village; and, indeed, such are all the places along here. These villages are not like those in the iron counties, as I call them; that is, the counties of flint and chalk. Here the houses have gardens in front of them as well as behind; and there is a good deal of show and finery about them and their gardens. The high roads are without a stone in them; and every thing looks like gentility.

So said William Cobbett, the journalist and social reformer, in his *Rural Rides*, published in 1830, but written in instalments in the 1820s, as a survey of contemporary rural conditions.

Rolvenden lies in the heart of the Kentish Weald, about half a dozen miles from the Sussex border and sixteen south-west of Ashford. It is still a beautiful and 'genteel' village, not that much changed since Cobbett's time; indeed, the population, 1,507 in 1831, was almost identical at the time of the 2001 census. Its name means 'Hrothwulf's woodland pasture', and it is recorded as 'Rovinden' in the Domesday Book of 1086. This version of the name has been retained in the correct modern pronunciation of 'Rovvinden', but by 1610 the current spelling had come into circulation. The picture is somewhat complicated by the temporary demise of the original 'Streyte' when it was almost completely burned down in 1665, the year of the Great Plague. The villagers moved a mile down the road to the common land of the 'Layne', an old dialect word for a large tract of arable land. They later returned to rebuild the Street, creating the two centres of population that survive to this day.

It was into this rustic scene that Edgar Willsher was introduced on 22 November 1828, the youngest of 14 children born to John and Charlotte Willsher. There is evidence of a Willsher family – the name incidentally has many variant spellings and simply means 'from Wiltshire' – living in Rolvenden from the sixteenth century, but the earliest inscription in the graveyard of St. Mary's, the parish church, relates to Stephen Willsher, 'yeoman', who died in

1785 at the age of 69. His marriage to Esther Catharine yielded 11 offspring, including another Stephen, father of John and therefore Edgar's grandfather, whom Edgar would never have met as the latter died in 1824.

The description of Stephen senior as a yeoman indicates a reasonable social status, as the yeomanry farmed their own land and could merge upwards into the gentry. The collapse of rural prosperity after the end of the Napoleonic wars more or less put paid to this class, and certainly, when John Willsher married Charlotte Winser in 1806, he was simply a 'farmer', and therefore not a property owner. Charlotte was also from a farming family in Tenterden, three miles north-east of Rolvenden, and at the time of Edgar's birth they had taken up residence at Little Halden Farm on the outskirts of the village.

The farm was owned by the local squire, Thomas Monypenny, who, on his accession to the ancestral estate at Hole House in Rolvenden in 1836, added Gybbon as a prefix in honour of a female ancestor of that name whose family owned Hole House before she married a Monypenny at the beginning of the eighteenth century. Gybbon-Monypenny's importance as a landowner was reflected in his election as Member of Parliament for Rye in 1837, although he appears not to have made a speech during his four-year tenure.

The tithe awards of the 1830s show John Willsher farming just over 160 acres, a not inconsiderable area, but small enough to be looked after by him and his large family, although by this time it had been reduced by the death of five of the children. By 1841 the census shows that the Willshers had moved down the road to the imposing Chessenden House, sharing with another farmer of advanced years and his 54-year-old daughter. Soon after that, the family moved again, this time travelling the ten miles to Goudhurst, where John died in 1843.

At the time of his death at the age of 61, John is described as an innkeeper, although it is unknown which hostelry he ran. Whether he simply felt it was time to retire, or whether other factors induced him to leave farming, it is impossible to say. Certainly, the 1830s saw the emigration of about 200 people from Rolvenden, partly due to the 'Swing Riots' that started in Kent in 1830, acts of vandalism targeting in particular the new-fangled threshing machines that were seen as a severe threat to the livelihoods of agricultural labourers. Little did young Edgar know of the rapidly changing times of which he would soon be a part.

Origins

Little Halden Farm, Rolvenden in 2010.
Edgar Willsher was born here on 22 November 1828.

Chessenden House, Rolvenden in 2010.
The Willsher family lived here in the early 1840s.

Only a few snippets have been handed down to us about his childhood. Arthur Haygarth, cricket's most assiduous chronicler, tells us that he first learnt the game from his brothers when eight or nine. In the first edition of his *Cricketers' Companion*, published in 1865, John Lillywhite says that 'when seven years old he bowled round arm to his brother in an apple orchard – a tree for wicket, home-made bat, and a wooden ball, and kept at it during winter in an old shed.' Therefore, despite the minor difference in age, the two accounts are in essence identical, and this is not surprising given the fact that Haygarth got the cricketers themselves to fill in a form with their biographical details. His brother William, fourteen years his senior, would have been his main mentor, assisted by George, just three years older. Both would play club cricket with him in later years.

The same sense of authenticity is not attached to another 'fact' buried in the written record. Lord Harris, who captained Edgar towards the end of his career, twice wrote that 'it is said' that he had only one lung from boyhood, but without independent corroboration it is impossible to know. It is a shame that the social conventions of the time precluded the future Governor of Bombay from asking Willsher, a lowly professional, directly. If he did only have one lung, his marathon bowling spells would have left him short of breath, but if he had trained himself to cope from childhood, they would certainly not have been impossible.

Edgar must have received a reasonable education, as he was quite capable of penning articulate letters to the newspapers in adulthood. In 1833, the first government grants were made for the setting up of church schools, and Rolvenden benefited with the founding of its own seat of learning in 1837. Elementary education was not yet compulsory, but if Edgar did attend school it would have been here, although no pupil records survive from this time.

Edgar's cricketing education, begun at home from an early age, would also have been enhanced by the visits of some of the county's greatest cricketers to the locality. A particularly notable occasion was the game in July 1835 between Benenden and Kent at Hemsted Park, home of Twisden Hodges, the local M.P. The Park, now owned by Benenden School, was only a three-mile walk from Little Halden Farm, so it is more than likely that the six-year-old and his brothers would have formed part of the crowd of 'at least 6,000'. Both the great allrounder Alfred Mynn and his brother Walter were playing, alongside the Wenman brothers and the legendary batsman Fuller Pilch. Edward Wenman was regarded as the best wicketkeeper of his day, and both he and his brother William were born and brought up in Benenden, so Edgar had very local heroes to admire. A decade or so later, he would be playing with all these great players, first in club cricket and later for Kent itself.

Amhurst Place, Upper Fant Road, Maidstone, birthplace of John Edgar Willsher, Edgar and Sarah's first child.

Chapter Two
Moving On

The move to Goudhurst appears to have progressed Edgar's cricket further as, according to Haygarth, he played regularly for the 'Boy Eleven' against local village teams, although contemporary newspapers are silent in this regard. However, in order to attract the notice of the county's cricketing establishment, he would need to move closer to one of its two major centres, Maidstone or Canterbury. Willsher's arrival in Goudhurst coincided with the shifting of the county team's activities from West Malling to the Beverley Club's ground in Canterbury in 1841, but high-class club cricket in and around Maidstone was set to flourish over the next decade, so either location would provide him with the opportunities he needed.

Whether or not it was to further Edgar's (and his brothers') ambitions, the family did move, plumping for Maidstone. By the next census, in 1851, Edgar was living at 52 Maginford, on the outskirts of Mote Park, with his mother, brother William, sister Charlotte and nephew John Lipscombe. William was working as a farmer's bailiff, and Edgar as a farm assistant, but he would not be helping out at home for much longer, and ten years later he was recorded for the first time as a professional cricketer. Haygarth says that the family moved to Maidstone in 1845, and this is about right, for in 1847 he finally received attention from the local press for his performances for a new club just two miles east of the town centre.

On 31 May 1847, at the age of 18, Edgar made his debut on the public stage, playing for Bearsted against Aylesford on Bearsted Green.[1] Although he scored only four and three, he bowled seven victims in the match, and may have taken more wickets that went unrecorded, as catches were still credited only to the fielder in some scorecards of the time. Bearsted, after a disastrous first innings of 20, rallied sufficiently to win by 36 runs. It was a family affair, as, in addition to a haul of seven wickets, brother William made a match-turning 42 not out, as he and Walter Mynn took the game away from Aylesford in the second innings. It was a most

---

1   *Maidstone Journal*, 1 June 1847.

satisfactory start.

Edgar's other cricketing brother, George, had first been recorded by the *Maidstone Journal* playing twice in 1846 for Staplehurst, equidistant between Maidstone and Rolvenden. The loose club affiliations of the time, and the lack of major matches, are demonstrated amply by the next sighting of Edgar, turning out himself for Staplehurst against Southborough at the beginning of July 1847. No wickets and six runs represented a poor return, but George more than made up for it with eleven wickets and 18 runs. The Willshers were on the march.

Recognition of the brothers' rapid rise was soon forthcoming for, on 15 July, William was picked to play for Kent against Surrey at the Preston Hall ground in Aylesford. It was the second and last 'important' match to be staged there under the aegis of the local Milner family, who used spurious names such as the 'New Kent Club' and the 'West Kent Cricket Club' in their attempts to promote the setting up of a county club to play matches home and away against Surrey. The ramifications of the long-running rivalry between the east and west of the county will be dealt with later, but suffice to say that, despite an easy Kentish victory in front of a large crowd, it proved to be the last time either Aylesford or William Willsher featured at this level of the game. With Alfred Mynn and medium-pacer William Hillyer taking all the wickets, Willsher was not called upon to bowl, and bagged an ignominious 'pair' down at number eleven. Obscurity beckoned, and it was to be another three years before Edgar had a chance to redeem the family name.

In volume four of his monumental *Scores and Biographies*, the essential tool for the early cricket researcher, Haygarth states that in fact Edgar, not William, first played for Kent in 1847 (in this match), but he retracts this in a later volume and confirms his county debut as 1850. Modern statisticians[2] now accept this, but the earlier date still slips through occasionally, even in Ric Sissons' excellent history of professional cricketers, *The Players*. Romantic as it might be to go with 1847, Edgar at 18 had simply not achieved enough to be selected for his county, but that was to change quite dramatically over the next two summers. His local reputation was to reach such heights that he could no longer be ignored, and once he was in the Kent side he was rarely to be left out as long as he was available.

---

2   See www.cricketarchive.co.uk for details of the games involved. The *Wisden* report of Willsher's benefit match at Lord's in 1871 repeats the inaccurate story of his 1847 appearance for Kent.

The 1848 season came and went with only two recorded appearances, one for Staplehurst against Tenterden, the other for Bearsted against Matfield Green, a small village near Tonbridge. 1849 was much busier, or at least the press took more notice, for Edgar is mentioned as playing in at least seven matches. The season slowly came to life in June with a drawn game for Bearsted in Chatham, with all three Willshers in the eleven. Edgar bowled nine of the opposition, including seven in the first innings, a feat suitably celebrated at the White Hart Inn, where, according to the *Maidstone Journal*, 'good harmony and "We won't go home till morning" were literally the order of the day.'

Edgar recovered sufficiently from the night's carousing to play two more matches for Bearsted in July, home and away against Stilebridge. There is still a Stile Bridge Inn near Marden, about ten miles south of Maidstone, which would explain why the *Kentish Gazette* changes the team name to Marden for its visit to Bearsted. However that may be, Edgar's golden form continued with six wickets in the first innings of the away fixture. The *Gazette* proclaimed that his bowling was, 'as usual, splendid, and the Stilebridge men, celebrated for hard hitting, found it difficult to cope with.' When the teams repaired to Bearsted Green, 'Marden' 'could not stand before the out-and-out bowling of the Willshers, Edgar alone having levelled six wickets ... in the first innings.'

In August, there was to be a further six-wicket haul at Chilston Park, ten miles east of Maidstone, but the apex of Edgar's season came in September when he agreed to take on two cricketers from Aylesford in a single-wicket match.[3] These were very popular with contemporary audiences, and in essence were similar to a back-garden knockabout, in that one batsman at a time defended one set of stumps, and only runs in front of the wicket counted. There could be one or several players on each side, but however many there were it was essential that they possessed at least a modicum of allround ability. Edgar certainly did, and his top score for the season was 26 at a time when, at this level of the game, team totals in three figures were the exception rather than the rule. Unfortunately, he failed to score, but he did bowl out both his opponents in the first innings. His colleague's 14 was enough to set up an innings victory, and to dissuade the Aylesford men from playing a return match at Bearsted!

---

3   *Maidstone Journal*, 11 September 1849.

Chapter Three
The Big Time

Those aficionados increasingly wearied by the ever-more congested modern fixture list will be relieved to learn that Kent played a mere six matches in 1850, three of them against England. The concept of a county championship was a long way off at this point in the game's history, with only a few inter-county matches played each year, resulting in a 'champion' declared annually by the press. The Wealden counties of Kent, Surrey and Sussex dominated the scene, with only Nottinghamshire really challenging from the north.

As it happened, the end of the 1840s coincided with the decline of the Kent side that can justly lay claim to being the greatest of all county elevens, the team immortalised in William Prowse's famous tribute, first published in 1861:

> Every man of the Eleven glad and proud to play his part;
> And with five such mighty cricketers, 'twas but natural to win
> As Felix, Wenman, Hillyer, Fuller Pilch and Alfred Mynn.[4]

In addition to those already mentioned, Nicholas Wanostrocht, or 'Felix' as he liked to be known on the cricket field, was only marginally inferior to Pilch as a batsman, and was a great thinker on the game, as seen in his classic tome *Felix on the Bat*, where he describes the ingenious bowling machine he called the 'catapulta'. Finally, William Martingell, an export from Surrey, provided excellent medium-paced support to Mynn and Hillyer. This mighty combination was more than a match for all-comers from the mid-1830s to the end of the 1840s, and indeed Kent were acclaimed in the press as champion county six of the seven years between 1837 and 1843. (No reference has been found to a team being chosen in 1840.)

By 1850, the team was ageing and in dire need of fresh blood. The time was ripe for young 'Ned' Willsher to be given his opportunity, and after impressing a crowd of 2,000 playing for Bearsted at the Beverley Club in Canterbury at the end of June, the call finally came. After a good start to the season, with a draw and a win against Sussex, it was decided to experiment for the

---

4   From his poem, In Memoriam, reproduced in Morrah, p.207 and elsewhere.

Surrey fixture by handing Willsher his debut and recalling the left-arm fast bowler Edmund Hinkly. The latter, like Wenman born in Benenden, was already 33, but had only started playing for Kent in 1846. In 1848, in his first appearance at Lord's, he amazed onlookers by taking all ten wickets in England's second innings, a feat unparalleled at the time. He almost repeated it in the corresponding fixture at Canterbury in 1849, but this time he had to content himself with a mere eight victims. On the face of it, Hinkly was the natural successor to Mynn and Hillyer as leader of the attack, but, like a comet, he flared brilliantly but all too briefly, and it would increasingly be left to Willsher to take on the mantle.

Willsher at the start of his Kent career.

So it was that Edgar set foot on The Oval's hallowed outfield for the first time on 11 July. He was to be the ninth of ten bowlers used as a fine Surrey side rattled up 246 by the close of the first day. Despite the match situation, he could be pleased with his efforts. With four wickets, he was the most successful bowler of the ten used, although we do not know his full analysis. However, this promising performance passed without fanfare, *Bell's Life* merely noting that he was 'a young player'. Kent's first innings was an inglorious 52, and Willsher, not out for nought at the end, must have kept his pads on, as he was asked to open in the follow-on. He batted stoically for eight, but it made little difference as a crushing innings defeat loomed. After such a start, it was unsurprising that Edgar found himself in the 'squad' of 14 to play England at Cranbrook, only six miles from his birthplace. In the end, he was denied a happy homecoming, and had to console himself with a game for Stilebridge instead.

As implied above, the mid-nineteenth century sporting press, whilst regaling its readers with frequent classical allusions and assessments of those of the 'fairer sex' in attendance at big matches, is rarely very helpful when it comes to judging a player's performance or ability. Thus it is worth including a particularly prescient comment from *The Era* concerning Edgar's appearance for Bearsted against East Kent that year:

> We like to be early in noticing talent, regardless of the quarter from which it may come. The match ,,. affords us an opportunity of introducing a family of cricketers, all of

whom, in a greater or lesser degree, are buds of promise; the name of Willsher will hereafter become as familiar to the lovers of cricket as household words.

Chapter Four
Methods

It may be appropriate at this point to take stock and consider what qualities as a cricketer Edgar possessed that made him 'a bud of promise', who would more than fulfil *The Era*'s prediction in sustaining a hugely successful career over a quarter of a century. Such longevity in itself was remarkable for a pace bowler, but there is also the small matter of how he managed to take 1,290 first-class wickets at an average of 12.78, in addition to 39 wickets for which no analyses have been preserved.

For pace bowler he certainly was; already in 1849 the *Kentish Gazette* was calling him 'fast', and this was a verdict confirmed by his contemporaries. Richard Daft, the classy Nottinghamshire batsman whose career stretched from 1858 to 1891, said in his 1893 book *Kings of Cricket* that he had 'tremendous pace', whilst the great allrounder William Caffyn, who played for Surrey from 1849 to 1873, said 'he was not so fast as either Jackson or Tarrant'. John 'Foghorn' Jackson of Nottinghamshire, and George 'Tear 'em' Tarrant of Cambridgeshire, together with Yorkshire's George Freeman, were the most celebrated bowlers of express pace in Willsher's day, and so to be talked of in the same breath in terms of speed indicates that Willsher was genuinely quick. To put it in context, although we cannot be sure of the velocity of bowlers from 150 years ago, a 'fast' bowler in the modern game such as Andrew Flintoff will regularly reach speeds of just over 90 miles per hour, while a 'very fast' bowler will touch 95 or above.

In his biography of Fred Spofforth, the 'demon' Australian bowler, Richard Cashman estimates that he bowled at about the pace of Alec Bedser (a maximum of fast-medium), because he regularly had batsmen out stumped. This may well be the case, but in the slightly earlier era in which Willsher played, all wicketkeepers stood up to the stumps, so pace cannot be judged by quite the same criteria. Even Jackson had batsman stumped off his bowling, but this does not necessarily mean that he was not 'fast'. Because of the unpredictable nature of the wickets, wicketkeeping in the middle of the nineteenth century was a lottery, and there would always be a longstop, very often one of the more able fielders, near the boundary as back-up. Bowlers like Jackson and Willsher would occasionally get batsman out stumped,[5] but there must have been at least as many occasions when the ball eluded the keeper and was retrieved by the longstop. No doubt Willsher's pace seemed greater in his day because of the treacherous conditions, and the fact is that he bowled as fast as he needed to in order to take wickets.

The secret of Willsher's success, however, lay in more than just his pace. Caffyn, referring to Jackson and Tarrant, opines that 'his ball was a more difficult one than those of either of those famous cricketers'. He goes on to say that he moved the ball a good deal from leg to off, 'and he seemed to have the knack of being able to make a ball "get up" on almost any wicket.' Writing in *Cricket* magazine, again in 1893, Daft gives us our best insight into exactly how this was achieved:

> He came up to the wicket with a quick-march kind of step; raised his hand high above his head, bringing it down, however, with a very quick jerky movement just as he delivered. That last movement of his seemed to put a spin on the ball that caused it to rise like lightning from the pitch. It seemed to reach one almost before it left his hand sometimes. I always found that I could play back more successfully than forward, although until one got used to him it was difficult to believe this could be done. Willsher was always a bowler that one was glad to see taken off if one were batting against him, and were well set even. One never knew what might happen, as he had so many nasty balls 'up his sleeve' which often produced disastrous results.

The Laws of Cricket at the time of Willsher's county debut stated that the bowler's arm had to stay below shoulder height in delivery, and this was to prove the bane of Willsher's professional life. However, we are not concerned with the height of his arm at this stage of the story, but the fact that bowling could at most be round-arm in 1850 meant that, because of the angle involved, the majority of its practitioners bowled from round the wicket. We do not have specific information on Willsher, but, assuming he also adopted this line of attack, it would have accentuated the difficulty of playing what was essentially a fast leg-break to the right-handed batsman. Combined with the extra bounce that his action seemed to generate, and the under-prepared state of contemporary wickets, the batsman would assuredly have felt

---

5   Willsher obtained 28 wickets by stumpings, some perhaps in matches where he reverted to traditional under-arm 'lob' deliveries, and Jackson 11.

that he was at times unplayable. It is interesting that he generated movement through spin, rather than swing. This seems to have been the technique in use through most of the nineteenth century, with right-arm bowlers spinning the ball from the off and left-arm bowlers like Willsher spinning it from the leg. The innovation of swing, or 'swerve' as it was known, does not really appear to have taken off until the last years of the century, although curiously Edmund Hinkly is said by Caffyn to have been one of its early exponents.

So Edgar had pace, bounce and movement, but allied to all these were phenomenal accuracy and consistency. Year after year he wheeled away à la Derek Shackleton (although the Hampshire man was never *fast*), hardly bowling a bad ball and sending down maiden after maiden. His most extraordinary feat of economy was for the All-England Eleven against an eighteen of Manchester Broughton in 1861, when he bowled 100 consecutive balls for just one run. Shackleton is renowned for taking 100 wickets in a season twenty times in a row between 1949 and 1968, but he played during an era of many more county matches than were available to Willsher. At the peak of his career between 1857 and 1871, the latter played about the same number of first-class matches[6] in a season as a twenty-first century county professional, and 50 wickets is now deemed to be the modern equivalent of a 100-wicket season's haul. Over that period, he only twice took fewer than 50 wickets in a season, and in one of those, 1858, he made just six first-class appearances.

Whilst figures can never tell the whole story, the statistician does have some useful tools at his disposal. With regard to a bowler's accuracy, runs conceded per 100 balls (economy rate) is the standard measure, while potency can be assessed by looking at the number of balls bowled per wicket (strike rate). Using these parameters, Willsher had an economy rate of close to 31 and a strike rate of just over 41. Bat now dominates ball to a much greater extent than in that far-off era, so a good economy rate for any style of bowler (including spinners) is considered to be anything less than 50, while a strike rate of under 50 in Test cricket is outstanding. Returning to our earlier example, Shackleton, like Willsher operating in the days of uncovered wickets, and therefore in less batsman-friendly conditions than exist today, managed a similar economy rate (34), but a strike rate of only 56.

The most useful comparisons are of course with Willsher's

---

[6] In compilations based on the ACS list of first-class matches.

contemporaries, and I set out below a table looking at a small selection of his peers. I have chosen the three great speedsters mentioned above, plus Tom Emmett of Yorkshire, perhaps, after Willsher, the greatest left-arm fast bowler of the time; Alfred Shaw of Nottinghamshire, renowned for his extreme miserliness with the ball; and the slow bowler James Southerton, whose career almost completely overlapped with Willsher's. For convenience the table is laid out in order by start of playing career:

Bowler	Career	Wickets	Avge	E.R.	S.R.
E.Willsher	1850-1875	1329	12.78	30.96	41.10
J.Southerton	1854-1879	1682	14.43	35.22	40.97
J.Jackson	1855-1867	655	11.52	35.96	32.04
G.F.Tarrant	1860-1869	421	11.89	36.01	33.01
A.Shaw	1864-1897	2027	12.13	24.10	50.32
G.Freeman	1865-1880	288	9.84	27.76	35.47
T.Emmett	1866-1888	1572	13.55	35.44	38.25

Notes: Economy rate (E.R.) refers to runs conceded per 100 balls, and strike rate (S.R.) to balls bowled per wicket taken.   Source: www.cricketarchive.com.

While clearly far from a comprehensive or scientific survey, we can at least see that Edgar was a match for any of his peers. Only Shaw and Freeman have better economy rates, and only Freeman is superior on both penetration and economy. The latter's incredible figures were also achieved over a much shorter career of 44 first-class matches. Whilst Willsher's strike rate is not as impressive as that of Jackson, Tarrant or Freeman, it is still competitive, and vastly superior to Shaw's, although he was a different sort of bowler. It should be noted that Southerton, Shaw and Emmett all played in the first-ever Test match in Melbourne in March 1877, and we can be certain that the 'Lion of Kent', as Daft and others liked to call him, referring to his position as the successor to the title once held by Alfred Mynn, would have been invited to take part if he had still been available.

From surviving photographs and descriptions, Willsher seems to have had a fragile physique, so he must have been stronger than he looked. In 1865, at age 37, he gave his height as 5 ft 11 in and his weight as 11 st 3 lb, which gives him, in modern terminology, a Body Mass Index of 21.9, well within the 'normal' range between 18.5 and 24.9, but many of his fellow players, like Sussex's John Wisden, 11 st 4 lb at just 5 ft 4½ in, returned an 'overweight' BMI, of 26.9 in his case. Lord Harris saw Willsher as 'an attenuated, consumptive-looking man' while Daft preferred the word 'cadaverous'. Caffyn, on the other hand, while agreeing that 'when in ordinary clothes he had not at all the appearance of an athlete', said that he had 'a very dark complexion'! This could perhaps be down to the then fashionable Abe Lincoln-style beard he sported for much of the second half of his career. However that may be, the fact that he pretty much walked up to the crease when bowling would have saved a lot of energy, and enabled him to keep going for long spells. There are certainly no records of injuries through his whole career, although there are occasional illnesses. He may of course have been stronger and more durable than he looked due to working on the family farm as a young man. W.G.Grace, in his book *Cricket* published in 1891, says that Willsher was 'past his best' when he first played against him; but he noted that 'he walked quietly up to the crease when delivering the ball, and yet was able to bowl fast.' His deliveries, in Grace's description, 'twisted in from the leg'.

Lord Harris is also very disparaging about Edgar's supposed lack of cricketing nous, claiming that:
> I do not think he had much idea of the science of the game, and beyond his own bowling never struck me as taking much interest in it … he had a curious, far-away look in his eyes, and used to look up at the sky as one talked to him.

While photographs do tend to suggest a 'far-away' look, there is the possibility that Willsher may have been cross-eyed, explaining the fact that he appeared to be looking elsewhere when addressed. An alternative reason may be simply that, when listening to someone who could be as autocratic and overbearing as Lord Harris, the best policy was to avoid eye contact! Edgar must have had more between his ears than his Lordship suggests, as he held many positions of responsibility throughout his life, including the coveted England captaincy in 1868. He also mounted an eloquent defence of his bowling action when push came to shove at the end of the 1850s.

At least Harris conceded that Willsher could bat,[7] and indeed 5,089 first-class runs at an average of 12.41 put him in the allrounder category for his times. Just as he was a wicket-taker who could bowl defensively, so he was also 'a fine hitter' who 'had an excellent defence as well.' Indeed Caffyn puts him among the great 'stonewallers', recalling his innings of 20 in nearly four hours playing for Kent and Surrey against England in 1855. Trevor Bailey himself would have been proud, and several times in his

---

[7] Like his bowling, left-handed.

career Willsher joined the great 'barnacle' among the élite group of cricketers who have opened both the batting and bowling in the same match. It was not until the last eight years of his career that his name regularly appeared in the lower half of the batting order in first-class cricket. At the start of his career, he was seen as almost equally promising with both bat and ball, and it is to that expectant era that we must now return.

Chapter Five
With the All-England Eleven

By the 1840s, something of a communications revolution was going on. Many of the railway routes to London had opened up, dramatically cutting average journey times, and the written word could now be transmitted much more speedily with the introduction of the Penny Black and the increasing use of telegraphy. Cricket was a major beneficiary, as matches could be more easily arranged and attended and also reported, in journals such as *Bell's Life in London*. Legislation was slowly allowing the ordinary worker more leisure time, culminating in the Factory Act of 1850, which obliged textile mills to close at 2 pm on Saturday. In addition to increasing the potential participants in, and audience for, a range of sports, these developments reflected a new belief in the benefits of manly exercise, and a delight in progress that saw its apotheosis in the Great Exhibition of 1851. The time was ripe for the expansion of the professional game, and all it required was a man with some entrepreneurial vision to help that come about.

Enter William Clarke, a rotund, one-eyed, 47-year-old lob bowler from Nottingham. His idea was to take an itinerant eleven of the best available cricketers around the country to play local teams consisting of up to 22 men. Given that until Clarke came along there had not been enough top cricket to make a full-time living, the scheme was attractive to both established and up-and-coming players. Members of the team could earn perhaps £5 for a big match, riches compared with an average labourer on 30 shillings a week, and Clarke made sure that there was a packed fixture list to keep his charges busy. The original team, unofficially dubbed the 'All-England Eleven' (AEE), played its first matches in 1846. In addition to Clarke, it contained such luminaries as Pilch, Mynn and Hillyer, to be joined in 1847 by Felix and the legendary trio of John Wisden and William Lillywhite of Sussex, and the young Nottinghamshire batsman George Parr, who later took over the reins from Clarke. Wisden and Parr were alone among this group in being born in the 1820s, and there would clearly be openings for younger, fitter individuals in the future. For the time being, however, Edgar needed to do more to establish himself in order to catch the gaffer's good eye.

The 1851 season started quietly for Ned, and he had to wait until the end of July for another call-up. Kent had lost both its previous matches, against England and Sussex, and decided to bolster its attack when England once again visited Cranbrook. The concept of 'England' was very much an unofficial one, but this time, extra complication was added by the fact that the side assembled here was Clarke's 'All-England' crew. It had become a tradition for 'England' to play the strongest county side, but Kent hardly merited the honour any longer. The match petered out into a draw, but Edgar acquitted himself well, taking three for 48 in the second innings. Even better was to come, as after missing the return match against Sussex, he had a further chance to impress against the 'national' side (not classified as 'All-England' this time, although still captained by Clarke and containing substantially the same players!) at Canterbury in mid-August. After a vital 24 batting at eight, he proceeded to rip the heart out of the England batting by bowling the impressive quintet of Guy, Box, Parr, Caffyn and Grundy, some of the leading lights of the day, later described in *Wisden* by W.H.Knight as 'a rare lot of wickets for a young hand to bowl down.' Unfortunately Parr had scored 54 by the time Willsher got rid of him, and England went on to win fairly comfortably, but a six-wicket haul finally 'established him as a bowler above the average.'

Unfortunately, 1852 saw him well *below* average, as he managed only five wickets in five games for Kent, although his batting kept him afloat, top-scoring with 30 opening the batting in an innings defeat against England at Canterbury in August. He was more successful in club cricket, taking 15 wickets in two matches for Stilebridge against Town Malling, and then finishing the season in style by taking five for 53 for an eighteen of Gravesend against the United England Eleven (UEE). This team, the brainchild of John Wisden and his Sussex colleague Jemmy Dean, was set up as a direct rival to Clarke's eleven, partly as a result of a falling out with the older man, but also as a business venture designed to capitalise on the fact that one travelling eleven was not enough to satisfy the hunger of the paying public for top-quality cricket. The Gravesend game was only the UEE's third out of four that season, but in 1853 it had a full fixture list. Willsher showed his willingness to travel by playing games for Stowmarket, Gentlemen of England (with three additional professionals), Maidstone and Ipswich against the UEE, taking 35 wickets in all. This was enough for the UEE to try him out themselves, and they must have been pleased with their investment, for in his third match, the last game of the season against 22 of Hampshire, he helped dismiss the opposition for 34 in a tight finish by taking 11 wickets.

Edgar had achieved recognition of sorts at the start of the season, being engaged as a net bowler by the gentlemen students of Oxford University, alongside other top professionals like Caffyn and Surrey's Julius Caesar. This was a good portent for the rest of the season, and he ended it with a highly satisfactory 21 first-class wickets in six matches at an average of 14.14. The biggest feather in his cap was appearing in the annual North v South match, one of the top two representative fixtures in these pre-international times, along with Gentlemen v Players. It was a quiet debut, as he was not required to bowl, but he did at least get to open the South's first innings with Julius Caesar. His old friends Hinkly and Hillyer bowled unchanged through both innings as the South cruised home by 70 runs. Everything was beginning to fall into place for Ned, and the final piece in the jigsaw was just about to be added. Clearly, his impressive performances both for and against the UEE had convinced William Clarke that he needed the Kent man's allround skills, and from 1854 Edgar became an All-England stalwart, never to play regularly for its rivals again.

Chapter Six
At Enville Hall

Ned made sure he seized the opportunity with both hands, and played no fewer than 15 of the 23 AEE matches in 1854, all against odds. In the eleven matches in which he was called on to bowl, he took a total of 58 wickets, which may not seem a lot against teams of 18 or 22, but the fact was that Clarke tended to put himself on to bowl non-stop at one end, leaving his minions to fight it out for the remaining scraps from the other. Willsher, although now 25 and approaching his peak, was still the junior player, and had done enough for the time being to keep his place for the foreseeable future. The highlight for him was a fifteen-wicket match haul against Sleaford, along with a top score of 20 in the AEE's second innings.

There was a certain amount of resentment against Clarke for supposedly taking key players away from county matches, but this was far from the case for Willsher, as he assisted Kent in all four of its matches that year. The thriller of the season was the return game against Sussex at Gravesend, with the visitors, after Wisden had bowled all seven of his second-innings victims, scraping home by three wickets in pursuit of a target of 94. Willsher had contributed five for 41 off 39.3 four-ball overs, but hard as he tried, he could make no difference in this or any other county fixture, as all four were lost. He would have derived much greater satisfaction from his mid-season appearance for his home town against the AEE at Mote Park. Alfred Mynn made 42 to give Maidstone a first innings lead of 23, and then took two for 11 as the AEE collapsed at the second attempt. Willsher played a full part with four wickets in an easy ten-wicket victory.

Edgar continued to be a regular with the AEE in 1855 and 1856, and indeed his performances in minor matches continued to provide his bread and butter throughout his career. Willsher's schedule for July 1855 provides a perfect illustration:

2	Salisbury	AEE v 18 of South Wiltshire
5-7	Reading	AEE v 22 of Reading
9-10	Enville Hall	AEE v Earl of Stamford's 22

12-13	Melton Mowbray	AEE v 22 of Melton Mowbray
16-17	Lord's	Kent and Surrey v England
18	West Wickham	West Wickham v Surrey
19-21	Gravesend	Kent v Sussex
23-25	Did not play for Players v Gents	
26-28	Newark	AEE v 22 of Newark
30-31	Stamford	AEE v 22 of Stamford

Lillywhite's Guide, the foremost cricket annual of the 1850s, described his bowling against Sussex at Hove in 1855, when he took four for 58 and seven for 22 in a resounding Kent victory, as something that 'could not have been surpassed'. After a brilliant season in 1856, in which, for the first time, he was the leading first-class wicket-taker with 66 at 10.76,[8] the *Guide* went one better, calling him 'perhaps the most destructive bowler in England'. *Bell's Life* agreed, saying that he was 'more difficult to play this year than ever'. The ultimate accolade came in July of that year when, for the first time, he was selected to play for the Players against the Gentlemen at Lord's. In a pulsating finish, his clear head was crucial as he guided the Players to their target of 70 with two wickets to spare. His 8 not out was augmented by a handy match return of nine for 63 from 46 overs with the ball.

On 1 March, 1857, the world of cricket awoke to the following announcement in *Bell's Life*:
> It will be a source of great gratification to all our cricketing readers to learn that the two celebrated Elevens of England will at length appear on the same field in friendly contest.

The significance was that, with the death of cantankerous old Clarke at the end of the 1856 season, and the accession of the rather more amenable George Parr to the leadership of the AEE, there was no longer any reason why the two rival teams should not meet on equal terms at the game's headquarters. Willsher was among the names selected for the first match, and he would have been disappointed if this was not case, as he had now been co-opted onto the management committee. He was also on the committee of the newly revived Cricketers' Fund Friendly Society (CFFS), set up to help out professionals fallen on hard times, and it was for the benefit of this body that the inaugural encounter was played. A second match was then to be staged as a testimonial for the UEE's Jemmy Dean.

---

[8] In a modern compilation based on the ACS list of first-class matches.

In front of a crowd of at least 10,000, Edgar opened the bowling for the AEE after Wisden had won the toss and batted on a fine June morning at Lord's. In a close contest, the AEE triumphed by five wickets early on the third day, at which point the teams trooped off to the house of James Dark, the Lord's proprietor, for a lunch of roast beef and plum pudding. Edgar would already have been sufficiently fortified by his own performance, as he took seven wickets and scored 20, a feat he bettered in the second match in July with nine wickets, including a second innings five for 16, off 21 four-ball overs, thirteen of them maidens, as he helped skittle the UEE for 54. At least Dean could console himself with the fact that he carried his bat for 8 not out, and also received the tidy sum of 'upwards of £400' (about £20,000 today) from the gate. With a net £160 left over from the first match to swell the coffers of the CFFS, it was clear that both events had been a financial and sporting success.

Edgar made limited appearances for the AEE over the next two years, as he had been engaged by George Harry Grey, the seventh Earl of Stamford. As a young man at Cambridge, Grey had succeeded to the Enville Hall estate in South Staffordshire, and no doubt stunned his family by marrying the daughter of a shoemaker who had turned his head during his student days at Trinity College. Another diversion from his studies was cricket, and in 1846 he hired a private ground behind the town jail, two years before Fenner created the playing field that has now become synonymous with Cambridge. He had clearly gained a taste for staging his own matches on an estate which he was developing as an all-round public attraction, and in 1848 allowed Stourbridge to take on Worcestershire at the newly built Enville ground. Before long he had started his own team, and from 1854 to 1857 it regularly played host to both of the great travelling elevens. Naturally, he engaged top professionals to do the bowling, and for the first three years Lord Stamford had the services of the Nottinghamshire duo of fast bowler John Bickley and slow under-armer Cris Tinley. Clearly, Willsher's 13 for 50 in the 1856 AEE fixture was enough to convince the Earl to add him to his retinue.

Willsher certainly had some business acumen, for the terms were very reasonable for comparatively light duties. Instead of the constant travelling and uncertainty associated with the All-England Eleven, here was security and a regular abode for the season. We have no record of payment for 1857, but in 1858 he received £112 for six months work, even though he only played in one match. The basic rate was £100 between 1 May and 1 October,

Fading cricket match under way at Enville Hall in South Staffordshire, the home of the seventh Earl of Stamford. Willsher was engaged as professional here in the summers of 1857 and 1858.

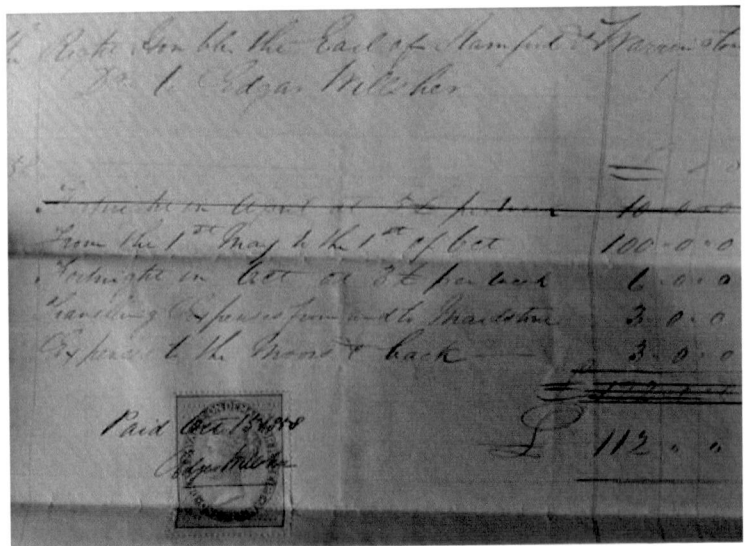

Extract from the accounts of the Stamford Estate showing payments of £112 to Willsher for his cricket services in 1858.

supplemented by payments for two weeks' work in October, and travel expenses to and from his home in Maidstone and 'to the moors and back'. Perhaps the latter refers to a day out on his Lordship's extensive grouse moors, something definitely not available to his AEE team-mates. He had been slightly busier in 1857, playing five matches at Enville Hall, and he was not entirely precluded from county cricket, joining Kent for all five of its fixtures. However, apart from his one game at Enville Hall against a twenty-two of Dudley, the month of August 1858 was devoid of cricket for Edgar, and he would have been especially keen to get back to Maidstone for a few days, especially if Stamford was paying, for he was now a married man.

The wedding took place on 24 February 1858 at St Saviour's Church in Southwark, consecrated as the cathedral in 1905, but having no obvious connection with either Edgar or his bride. Sarah Johnston was born at sea in 1826, the daughter of a quartermaster serving with an infantry regiment, the 67th South Hampshires. The Army Lists show John Johnston to have been receiving a daily subsistence of 4s 9d in 1823. 'The Tigers', as they became known, had been stationed in India since 1805 when George IV recalled them to England in 1826; hence Sarah's birth on board ship. The census of 1841 shows her living in Rolvenden and therefore presumably known to Edgar, but unfortunately she seems to leave no trace in the 1851 census. Quite apart from the marriage certificate claiming their residence as High Street, Southwark, further mystery is added by Edgar's profession being declared as 'victualler'. The solution may perhaps be found in the fact that Edgar's cousin Robert Willsher was the landlord of the Queen's Head in Borough at this time,[9] and it is therefore quite likely that Edgar and Sarah were helping out there in the winter of 1857/58. Whatever the reality of the situation, the birth of their first child, John Edgar, in April 1859, sees them happily ensconced back in Maidstone, and Edgar rightfully restored to the status of 'cricketer'.

The other momentous event in Willsher's life in 1859 took place at the Mitre Hotel in Maidstone on 1 March. Since 1841, the Beverley Club's ground had been the main centre for Kent cricket, especially after the founding of Canterbury Week in 1842. The problem was that the man in charge of the Week from 1849, William de Chair Baker, was seen as only being interested in the Kent County Club when it came to Canterbury, and therefore it was suffering

---

9   As recorded in the 1861 census.

as a whole from neglect. The Club was also losing money as a consequence of results on the field. Although Willsher had been joined by two fine bowlers in Fred Hollands and George Bennett, there were just not enough professionals of merit to uphold the county's high reputation. As a response to an increasingly desperate situation, the brothers Edward and Henry Bligh, uncles of Ivo, the 'Ashes' captain of 1882/83, called a meeting to sort out the mess. A new club was formed with a new committee that included players like Wenman and Alfred Mynn, and a new constitution that proposed taking power away from Canterbury by not having a regular ground and thus bringing the team to all parts of the county. Thus a solution was found for the moment, but whether the truce could hold was anybody's guess.

On the field the next three seasons were a golden era for Edgar, leading to a haul of 246 wickets at an average of 10.10 in just 43 first-class matches. Notable among his performances was that in the Gentlemen v Players match at Lord's in 1861, when he and Jackson, operating unchanged in both innings, destroyed the cream of amateur batsmanship. The six wickets he took in

The All-England Eleven of 1861.
Standing (l to r): E.Willsher, H.H.Stephenson, G.Parr, unidentified, T.Hayward, G.F.Tarrant, G.Anderson, R.C.Tinley, J.Jackson.
On the ground: A.Clarke, R.P.Carpenter.
In this year, Willsher played three matches for this side against the United England Eleven, at Lord's, Old Trafford and at The Oval.

this match were as nothing, however, compared with his virtuoso demonstration of the bowler's art at Canterbury on 13 August 1860. Playing for sixteen of Kent against England, he took eight for 16 off 41 overs, 31 of which were maidens; the feat earned him a collection of £8. They remained the best figures of his career. For once, the press was effusive in its praise. *Bell's Life* claimed that 'there are few who differ in opinion that he is the most difficult to play of any bowler in England', while *Baily's Magazine* opined that 'he never bowled better in his life'. *The Times*, on the other hand, was content to dwell on the amateur dramatics of the 'Old Stagers', whose amusing evening skits included the classic 'You Can't Marry Your Grandmother'. Whether Edgar attended or not, his high spirits would have been enhanced ten days later by the birth of a second son, Ernest. Both domestically and professionally, everything was going right for the Willshers, but such contentment was soon to be shattered by on-field events of seismic proportions.

Chapter Seven
'Willsher's Hand is Very High' [10]

Just after six o'clock on 26 August 1862, in front of a packed house of Ovalites, Edgar Willsher was no-balled for throwing by umpire John Lillywhite. Although Lord Harris reported that his father reckoned there was a 'fling' in Willsher's action, there was no real groundswell of opinion that he was, in the modern parlance, a 'chucker', but there was a general consensus that he regularly contravened Law 10. In effect, this allowed round-arm, but not over-arm, bowling, and it was for raising his arm above the shoulder that Edgar was now penalised. The ructions this caused in the cricket world will be discussed later, but first we need to go back in time to understand how it was that the 'Lion of Kent' came to be at the centre of a storm that had been brewing since the turn of the century.

Eighteenth-century laws of cricket make no specific mention of how the ball should be bowled, but we do know that originally the bowler rolled the ball along the ground, that is literally 'bowling' it. Some time before the nineteenth century, bowlers started to 'pitch' the ball underhand, thus leading to the straightening of the bat as the batsman now had to cope with the ball bouncing. So far so good, but the history of the game has seen a constant struggle for ascendancy between bat and ball, and, round about 1790, one man decided that the bowler's weaponry should be enhanced. Tom Walker, memorably described by John Nyren in *The Cricketers of My Time*, our primary source of information on the legendary Hambledon Club, was the man who 'began the system of throwing instead of bowling', meaning that he raised his arm perhaps up to his shoulder. The Hambledon Club seems to have quickly nipped this practice in the bud, but the early years of the new century saw the MCC, now the game's chief legislator, so concerned about the continuance of this 'menace' that it introduced for the first time a law that specified that 'the ball is to be bowled under-hand and delivered with the hand below the elbow.'

The main culprit at this time was John Willes, born at Headcorn near Ashford in Kent in 1778. The well-known story of his sister

---

10   'In Memoriam', line 1; see note 4 above.

Christina having to bowl round-arm to him because of her fashionably voluminous skirts is quite possibly true, but what *is* certain is that, having decided to bowl round-arm himself, John was not going to give up for anyone, attested to by his storming out of the Kent v MCC match at Lord's in 1822 after his mode of delivery was objected to. His contribution to cricket was not quite at an end, however, as a few years later he spotted the young Alfred Mynn playing locally and immediately recognised his talent, just as Mynn himself discovered Willsher two decades later. There were to be several more links in the chain, though, before Willsher finally brought bowling to something like its modern state.

Curiously, John Willes was an amateur, almost a traitor to the cause of tradition upheld by the gentlemanly membership of the MCC, but it was two professionals who continued to carry the torch for round-arm as the century wore on. William Lillywhite and Jem Broadbridge were at the forefront of the 'march of intellect', as the case for progress came to be known, and in 1827 it was finally agreed that a series of big matches would be used to test what, if any, advantage the new style gave the bowler. At the end of the second match, the reformers looked to be losing the argument, as nine of the England players signed a declaration to the effect that they would not play the final trial match 'unless the Sussex bowlers bowl fair – this is, abstain from throwing.' Fortunately, they later withdrew their complaint and England went on to win the final match, thus proving that round-arm did not offer too much of an advantage to the bowler. Ironically, one of the signatories, Tom Marsden of Sheffield, was himself no-balled for throwing while bowling at Nottingham at the end of August. The *Sheffield Independent* reported that, on leaving the field in protest, the Sheffield players 'were stoned and abused by the crowd.'

Double standards were a constant theme running through the disputes of the period, and the big issue that was largely ignored by the powers that be was the standard of wickets, especially at the game's headquarters. Naturally bowlers wanted to exploit any unevenness in the surface, whilst batsmen, both amateur and professional, were not keen on any development that might lead to greater risk of injury. Therefore, even after the law was finally changed in 1835 to allow bowling up to shoulder height, the rumblings of discontent continued. Lillywhite especially continued to push the boundaries of what was allowable, and was no-balled for 'bowling too high' for England v MCC at Lord's in 1839. No repercussions followed, and he presumably modified his action after the incident, as he continued to bowl throughout the match. The fact was that Lillywhite, despite being a leviathan of the game, was not quick enough to threaten the batsman's body with serious damage, and it was only when faster bowlers began to raise the height of their arms in the 1850s that a climax was finally reached.

Willsher was undoubtedly one of those faster bowlers who was seen as 'getting away with it' from early on in his career, but not everyone thought that his arm was too high at the point of delivery. Daft was, as ever, very supportive in this regard:

> He caused a great deal of bother by bowling unfairly, as was declared by many – that was, by delivery above the shoulder. ... I myself always thought that Willsher's delivery was within the limits of the old law, although it cannot be denied that to the spectators who did not watch him most closely he appeared to deliver above the shoulder. As a matter of fact, I believe that when the ball left his hand it was exactly on a level with his shoulder.

On the other hand, Caffyn, despite being an admirer of his old friend, sided with the majority in that 'there is no doubt whatever that Willsher was in the habit of bowling above the shoulder, but then so also were nine out of every ten bowlers of that time'. Even though Willsher was seen as the most flagrant abuser of Law 10, it was not he but a younger, rawer recruit whose action was the catalyst for a heated series of public exchanges in the first half of 1858.

The letters page of *Bell's Life* in the mid-Victorian era was the equivalent of an internet forum today, and thus reflected the immediate opinions of often anonymous correspondents, inevitably leading to personal abuse and indeed full-blown character assassination. In February 1858, the discussion centred around the singling out of the young Surrey allrounder George Griffith by 'A M'D', rather than other possible miscreants in the 'throwing' debate, such as Willsher. 'A Charitable Cricketer' wrote with some feeling that, as far as the noble game of cricket was concerned, 'if discussions upon its technical points cannot be entered into without personalities and party feeling, the sooner they are discontinued the better.' If this sentiment seems very familiar to the modern reader, we are also on well-trodden turf when we learn that Griffith, like Tom Marsden thirty years previously, had himself signed a petition against high bowling at the end of the 1857 season. The signatories included most of the UEE, including Wisden, Caffyn and John Lillywhite. The request was for a strict interpretation of Law 10 by umpires in important matches, since 'we find no individual who will take the responsibility upon himself to commence "no-balling" those who we are of opinion are unfair.'

The lawmakers of the MCC were entirely in accordance with the aims of the petition, and the ultra-conservative Robert Grimston, one of its staunchest committee members, proposed an addition to the law, so that a bowler could be no-balled if he raised his arm above the shoulder '*immediately preceding the delivery*'. 'A Charitable Cricketer' summed up the opinion of many when he wrote in a letter of March 1858 that 'there are many underhand bowlers even, who in *preparing* to deliver the ball raise the hand and arm above the shoulder', thus raising the ludicrous prospect of under-arm bowlers being no-balled under the new Law 10. He also suggested setting up an independent committee to consider all sides of the argument, but neither point cut any ice with the mandarins at Lord's, who duly passed the amendment with the minimum of fuss on 5 May.

Willsher himself stayed out of the debate until he felt his hand was forced by one 'Blink Bonny', a self-proclaimed 'professional cricketer' who felt compelled to name the most serious offenders of 'the present day'. Starting with Willsher, he was adamant that:
> this young cricketer (I will speak the truth and defy contradiction) four years since bowled as fair as Caffyn does at the present time, but in going round the country with the England Eleven, and playing on all kinds of grounds, he found the higher he got the more difficult he was to play. I did not hear a cricketer last season (a few Kent men excepted) but what said it was foul bowling.

Despite his protestations that his attacks were nothing personal, he named several other bowlers, including Willsher's Kent colleague Hollands – apparently 'higher' than Willsher – and John Lillywhite. According to the writer, the latter had also until recently bowled 'fair', and 'Blink Bonny' asserted that it would be easy for both him and Willsher to revert back to their former legitimate style.

Such accusations could not pass unanswered, and *Bell's Life* duly printed Willsher's rejoinder on 28 March. Having denied that his bowling had changed at all over the years, he goes on to say:
> I cannot imagine anything more degrading than the attempt to deprive his brother cricketers of their professional reputation. For my own part I intend to guard my own, as I do my wicket, at all events, from foul play ... Would

'Blink Bonny' like to face Jackson at Lord's when the ground is hard ... allow me to give a hint to the proprietors of grounds generally – to have a larger roller, and use it early and often, then you would not see the ball bound about in all directions as it does now.

As will be seen later in the story, Edgar was a great supporter of his fellow cricketers and their right to a decent living, and this betrayal by a 'brother' professional was beyond the pale in his eyes. The fact that it was anonymous was even worse, although Willsher implies that he knows who it is. There is certainly no doubt that the main target of his 'advice' is the MCC committee, whose intransigence delayed any kind of improvement in the Lord's wicket until the 1880s, when it introduced mechanical mowers and horse-drawn heavy rollers.

In the light of subsequent events, the response of John Lillywhite is even more intriguing. Writing in the same issue, he admits to bowling 'high' and continues:

... nothing will give me greater pleasure than for the umpire to 'no ball' me. I should then think he was taking a step in the right direction. Although a high bowler myself, no batsman was punished more than I was from it last season; balls flew over your head, and then, perhaps, one 'under the ear'. The public I am sure do not like to see it. Other bowlers must speak for themselves. I am in favour of the Hon R.Grimston's new rule, as I think it will do much good to cricket.

While almost acting as an 'undercover' agent for Grimston, Lillywhite is still implying that wickets were at fault as much as anything else, for such inconsistency of bounce was not apparent on the well-prepared surfaces found, for instance, at Enville Hall. Although on opposite sides of the argument, both he and Willsher were clear that any future action by a strong-willed umpire would ultimately lead to improvements in the standard of pitches, a development that would meet the approval of all those who played the game for a living; for the gentleman cricketer, used to having things his own way, it was to seem like the beginning of the end.

Chapter Eight
Incident at The Oval

The 1862 season saw a continuance of Willsher's good form, his most memorable contribution being a match figure of eight for 71 in the AEE's pulsating victory over the UEE at Lord's. A curiosity was his adoption of under-arm in Kent's clash with Surrey at The Oval in July. Having seen the success achieved by Surrey's wicketkeeper Tom Lockyer with his slow under-arm 'teasers' in Kent's disastrous second innings, Edgar decided to try some of his own when Surrey were left to chase a modest target. He took three for 44, but should have fared even better, as, according to *Bell's Life*, 'the field did not assist him properly'. The experiment was not continued, however, but there was to be one more big appearance at The Oval, this time playing for England against Surrey in the last important match of the season.

Having won the toss on a traditional Oval 'belter', England spent most of 25 and 26 August racking up an unprecedented 503, off 265 four-ball overs, in front of a crowd of at least 5,000. Willsher played his part, scoring 53 of an opening stand of 124, and by the time he came to open the bowling late on the second evening, he had had ample chance to put his feet up. After Willsher had bowled a maiden from the pavilion end, his captain, V.E.Walker of the famous Southgate brotherhood, followed suit from the other. In the fourth over, Walker's second, Humphrey was caught by Grundy for a duck, bringing the amateur Fred Burbidge to the crease. As the batsmen had crossed during the catch, Burbidge was therefore on strike when Willsher commenced his third over. What happened next was, at least temporarily, to make Edgar Willsher the most notorious cricketer in the land.

The first ball of the over was no-balled by John Lillywhite, standing at the bowler's end, and was despatched to the off-side boundary by Burbidge. After the next ball was also called, the crowd began to wonder what was going on. After all of the next four were called in the same flat voice, the bowler had had enough. Let *Sporting Life*'s reporter take up the story:

> Upon this, Willsher, instead of attempting to finish the over, naturally irritated and hurt at this unexpected proceeding

39

on the part of John Lillywhite, threw down the ball and walked towards the dressing-room, followed by the rest of the players. In an instant all was confusion and excitement. Cheers were raised for Willsher, and counter-cheers for Lillywhite, who remained in the field, till the time for drawing the stumps had arrived, surrounded by thousands of the spectators.

In fact, the two England amateurs, Walker and C.G.Lyttelton of Cambridge University, stayed on the field with Lillywhite, as they could not be seen to condone the intemperate acts of a bunch of professionals. Walker's biographer, Walter Bettesworth, later explained:

> When the incident happened he spoke to Willsher, who was, however, so exasperated and beside himself that he would not listen to reason, and walked away, the other professionals following him instantly. Now if the captain had gone after them to try to persuade them to return it is clear that this action would have been misunderstood. He would have given the impression that he was, like the professionals, leaving the field to express his feelings, and, although he might have returned, the mischief would have been done, and the effect would have been lamentable.

Bell's Life suggested that Willsher could have finished the over by bowling under-arm, and Walker himself claimed that, if he had known that Lillywhite intended to no-ball the Kent man, he would have put him on at the other end where Tom Sewell senior was presiding. This certainly worked for Arjuna Ranatunga when Muttiah Muralitharan was no-balled by Darrell Hair at Melbourne's Boxing Day Test of 1995. Just as in 1862, the crowd at first had no idea what was going on when Hair started no-balling Muralitharan, but after seven calls it was perfectly clear. Ranatunga went off to consult the match referee and duly moved his prize bowler

---

X. The ball must be bowled. If thrown or jerked, or if the Bowler in the actual delivery of the ball, or in the action immediately preceding the delivery, shall raise his hand or arm above his shoulder, the Umpire shall call "No Ball."

Law 10 as enacted at the time of The Oval incident, from a contemporary handbook. Its equivalent in the fourth edition of the 2000 code, Law 24, has some 400 words relating to 'fair delivery and the arm', including 'Underarm bowling shall not be permitted except by special agreement before the match.'

Incident at The Oval

These pages from the Surrey scorebook cover the county's first innings against England in August 1862 when Willsher was no-balled six times by John Lillywhite. The absence of ball-by-ball entries on the bowling page suggests that it was 'copied up' afterwards.
(Courtesy of Surrey History Centre.)

down the other end, where the rest of his spell passed off without incident. So Walker missed a trick by not consulting with the authorities, but Willsher was also at fault, as according to *Sporting Life*, Lillywhite had warned him in the previous over and he had carried on regardless.

The immediate problem was how to get the England players back on the field. The president of the Surrey club, George Marshall, chaired an impromptu committee meeting in the pavilion, the upshot of which was to keep Lillywhite as umpire but allow Willsher to bowl as normal for the rest of the match. Naturally enough, Lillywhite refused their kind offer, and he was replaced for the third day by George Street, a minor cricketer who had never played top-class cricket, and would thus not cause any trouble. At this news, says the *Sporting Life*, Willsher expressed his 'deep regret for the part he had taken in the affair', and indicated that England were now willing to continue the match. The Surrey committee 'courteously declined to claim the game, which of course they were entitled to.' The crisis was thus averted, and further action would have to wait until after the match, but at last the issue of 'high' bowling would have to be resolved one way or another. Whilst joining in the universal chorus of praise for Lillywhite's courageous stand in enforcing the letter of Law 10, *Sporting Life* left its readers in no doubt over its preferred outcome:

> The law, as overridden by the late style of bowling, is practically obsolete ... if ... the law can be so framed as to make the bowling of Willsher and a host of our very best cricketers *legally* available against the superior batting of the present day, so much the better.

Particular umpire. John Lillywhite in 1859.

The question remains as to why Lillywhite chose this particular match to make his point. Bearing in mind his letter from 1858, it was clearly something he had felt strongly about for some time, and if, as Walker claims, he 'had never previously acted as umpire', then it would make perfect sense. The trouble is that this assertion is incorrect. Indeed, the first first-class match he umpired was back in 1856, when Willsher took, in all, 11 wickets for Kent and Sussex against England at Lord's. Lillywhite would therefore have had ample opportunity to take a look at him then, and the importance of the occasion and the venue would have merited action. He also saw Willsher bowl 57 overs under his jurisdiction in the Gentlemen v Players match at The Oval in 1861, so the 1862 match was Lillywhite's third chance to call him.[11] It is perhaps understandable that he waited for the law change of 1858 to take action, but it is still a mystery as to why he did not do so in 1861. Perhaps this was the first time Willsher had bowled from his end. Lillywhite is said to have told Walker 'that he had often told Willsher that if he ever umpired in a match in which Willsher was bowling from his end he would "no-ball" him, unless he lowered his arm.' Ned seems to have thought that Lillywhite was joking, and this, combined with Lillywhite's correspondence in *Bell's Life*, suggests that there was no element of collaboration between the two old colleagues. Although both had a vested interest in reform of Law 10, their aims were very different. Unless Willsher was an extremely good actor, the indignation he felt at The Oval in 1862 was very real indeed.

The last day of the match started an hour late for no obvious reason, and, despite Willsher's best efforts, the time wasted prevented an England victory. There was no perceptible change in his delivery from the second day, but he of course remained unchallenged by either umpire, and swept aside the Surrey batting with six for 50. Following on 401 behind, the Londoners were hanging on grimly at 154 for six when stumps were drawn. Nobody had expected any major incidents after the drama of the day before, but, in the second innings, according to *The Era*, Willsher was 'groaned at by some beery, contemptible fellows, who knew as much about what they were grunting at as a pig, and we were delighted to see their "half and half" opinions drowned by the applause of the sensible portion of the visitors.' *Sporting Life* was equally indignant, defending Willsher as 'that worthy and inoffensive, but at the same time finished cricketer, Edgar Willsher, than whom no better fellow ever breathed.' Such demonstrations from the crowd were confined to this match, most punters realising that Willsher was not out to make trouble and was as keen as anyone for these momentous events to lead to long-lasting solutions. *The Era* was not alone in thinking that, instead of leaving the decision-making to the MCC, the answer was 'a Cricket Parliament, formed by the president and secretary of each County Club in existence *and* a

---

11   Lillywhite was, however, only 35 at the time of the incident, and in only his fifth first-class match as an umpire, according to modern compilations. He thus had no great seniority among the umpiring fraternity. He did not stand again in first-class cricket for another five years.

certain quota of the MCC.' Only by these means, it argued, could Law 10 be either struck off or rigidly enforced, and this was now a matter of the utmost urgency: 'bound up in its effective settlement is the very existence of the noble and national pastime of Cricket.'

Chapter Nine
Overarm at Last

At first, events moved fairly swiftly in the autumn of 1862. At the meeting of the influential Surrey committee on 17 October, it was resolved that 'a letter should be written by the secretary asking them [the MCC] to see a deputation regarding Law 10.' As far as the Law itself was concerned, the committee was of the opinion that 'with respect to bowling that a man should deliver as high as he liked so that he did not throw or jerk.' The letter clearly worked, for on 31 October the MCC decided 'that a Circular be drawn up and forwarded to the secretaries of the Principal Cricket Clubs respecting Law 10.' Although there was to be no Surrey deputation at Lord's, the counties were duly canvassed, and they voted by a majority of seven to three to remove all restrictions on the height of the arm. This was still not enough to sway the MCC, who came up with two unworkable compromises at a vital committee meeting in April 1863. Since neither of these was passed, and no other alternatives were produced, the Law was left to fester in its own juices for the whole of the 1863 season, with umpires under strict instructions to uphold it, and players warned to bowl high at Lord's at their peril.

Naturally, Willsher was under particular scrutiny, and great anticipation surrounded his first appearance at headquarters since 'the incident'. The occasion could not have been grander, as the game was the annual clash between the AEE and the UEE in May. When the UEE took first innings, the tension mounted when the ball was tossed to Willsher for the first time. *Bell's Life* takes up the story:

> The first ball delivered gave sufficient proof that he was not breaking the laws of the Marylebone Club; he was quite low, and no doubt lower than we shall see him again. He was also straight, in fact 'all there' ... this must have been most gratifying to the renowned Kent bowler and his friends.

The crucial test had been passed, allowing Edgar to breathe more easily, and six cheap wickets gave the lie to those who claimed he could only be a threat when he 'cheated'. Even Thomas Beagley, an ex-Hampshire professional from the 'old school', grudgingly accepted this when he wrote in *Boy's Own Magazine* in the same year that 'we know now that he can bowl good balls – perhaps with more spin and bias – when he bowls low.' *Bell's Life* provided a worrying footnote to its report of the match, won by the UEE by 70 runs, when it said that Law 10 'was not *strictly* enforced in one or two cases', so the situation was still no closer to being properly resolved.

Willsher had a decent enough season in 1863, taking 80 wickets in matches which we now treat as first-class. In spite, or perhaps because, of the controversy now surrounding his name, he had his best season with the bat, scoring 494 runs in seventeen matches at an average of 17.64 in a year when wickets cost 15.82 each. He recorded his highest score in first-class cricket, 89, batting at five in Kent's first innings at Sandgate Hill, near Folkestone, in only the second first-class match played on the ground.[12]

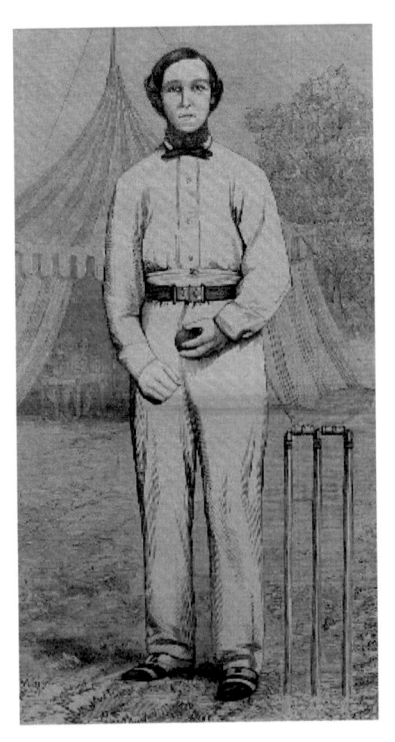

Willsher, aged 34, as pictured by the Illustrated Sporting News at the end of the 1863 season. Despite his 'faraway look' his seventeen first-class matches this year brought him 494 runs and 80 wickets.

---

12   His innings was the highest individual score in the match and it has remained the ground first-class record.

The legislative impasse may have lasted even longer if the MCC's new secretary, R.A.Fitzgerald, had not been appointed. A man of reforming zeal, the Cambridge-educated Fitzgerald took over in 1863 with the best of intentions, but, just like the art establishment, the cricketing hierarchy proved to be a tough nut to crack. Around the time of Fitzgerald's accession to the secretary's post, Edouard Manet's provocative *Déjeuner sur l'herbe* was being exhibited at the Salon des Refusés in Paris, and it was many years before its undoubted merits were accepted, paving the way for a whole series of modern artistic movements. In the same way, Fitzgerald found continued resistance to issues like the improvement of the Lord's playing surface, but in the matter of Law 10 at least, he could not be refused. At a meeting of 29 April 1864, Charles Marsham, a near contemporary of Fitzgerald's, brought before the MCC committee an amendment that said simply that 'the ball must bowled; if thrown or jerked the umpire shall call 'no ball.' Even at this stage, Robert Broughton, a Cambridge Blue in the 1830s, proposed yet another subtle variant of the existing Law, but enough was enough. On 10 June, part way through the season, and nearly two years after Willsher's no-balling, Marsham's amendment was passed 27 to 20, a majority of seven, after a debate in which about ten members spoke. Cricket's own modern age had begun, and perhaps the MCC recovered some of its authority within the game.[13]

There was a sense that at last the game had been allowed to evolve to its natural limits, and whether this was a good thing or not, there was a general feeling of relief that all the wrangling and uncertainty was over. Round-arm had been an unnatural state of affairs, as admitted by arch-traditionalist James Pycroft, one of the most eminent of Victorian cricket historians. Writing in *Cricketana* in 1865, he said:

> Keep your hand low and near your side as in the old style and your muscles play true and easily. Raise your hand above your head as Willsher does and as old Lilly used to do when he was deadly accurate and the muscles here also have some degree of satisfaction: but try to use the arm between these two points of elevation and you feel your disadvantage at once.

Although Pycroft still preferred the gentle rhythms of under-arm, he could at least see the advantages of over-arm, but one man at least was not prepared to budge. In the same year as *Cricketana*,

---

13   A subsequent MCC secretary, R.S.Rait Kerr, wrote in 1950 that the years '1840 to 1864 represent the very worst period of MCC control of the game'.

John Lillywhite launched the first edition of his *Cricketer's Companion*, the third section of which contains 'Hints on the Game':

> In commencing to bowl, never practise the high windmill sail delivery; it neither adds grace, effectiveness or pleasure to the game; ... The great secret to be obtained is, a delivery which will cause the ball to rise about bail-high, and possessing a good twist; and to arrive at this point of excellence, practise delivery about the height of the shoulder.

Reminiscing to A.W.Pullin ('Old Ebor') in the latter's *Talks with Old English Cricketers*, Walker emphasised that 'Willsher and Lillywhite were really very great chums, and they soon made up the little difference which this scene caused.' The 'little difference' might have become permanent if Edgar had known that his old friend had previously defended the bowling of Tom Wills, the controversial Australian. Wills was finally no-balled for throwing in 1872, but back in 1853 he attended Rugby School, where Lillywhite was cricket master at the time. There was doubt about Wills' action even then, and not just over whether he raised his arm too high. Correspondence in the pages of *Bell's Life* suggested that his arm was bent on delivery, an accusation to which Lillywhite felt he had to respond:

> I can only say that the bowling of Wills ... was perfectly fair, or the umpires at Lord's would have no-balled [him] ... I am professionally engaged by the school, and if gentlemen were less personal in their remarks ... they would do less injury to us cricketers.

Clearly Lillywhite's eyesight had improved immeasurably in the intervening decade!

It would have been natural for Edgar to feel rather bitter about the whole affair, but he seems to have borne it all with his usual stoicism. In the obituary of Willsher published in *Cricket* magazine, Robert Thoms, a leading contemporary umpire, said that he 'often pathetically remarked that he had been born too soon', and certainly his career was now half over. Yet, although he was now in his thirty-sixth year, and although Lord Harris thought that he was never the same bowler after 1862, his good form continued unabated in 1864, with 79 wickets at 13.48. This was despite having to modify his action, at least temporarily, in 1863. *Every Boy's Magazine* commented on 1 July that during the season Willsher 'had not apparently the same command or accuracy; but a low delivery gives more spin and therefore Willsher's "break back" (twist the reverse way) was very difficult.' When the need to keep his arm low was removed in 1864, the old accuracy returned, but with new tricks at his disposal. However, he never became a true over-arm bowler in the modern sense of the word, and his action, even after the law change, would have been similar to that of Mitchell Johnson at the start of the 2009 Ashes, with his arm not far above the shoulder in delivery. Most of his compatriots followed suit, to the extent that, when the 'demon' Spofforth first toured England in 1878, batsmen were literally bowled over, not just by his pace, but also by the unaccustomed height of his arm.

Further evidence that Willsher and Lillywhite soon buried the hatchet[14] comes in a notice from the *Sporting Gazette* of 26 November 1864:

>An important meeting of the professionals of the south of England was held at the Bridge House Hotel, London Bridge, November 17 ... the appearance of so many of the 'cracks' at the Bridge House at this time of the year caused a little commotion. John Lillywhite was voted to the chair, Edgar Willsher to the vice chair. After a long discussion, in which each 'had a say', it was resolved unanimously that the eleven be called 'The United South of England Eleven'.

Willsher was voted in as secretary, and Lillywhite as treasurer, a proposal seconded by Edgar himself. The meeting was attended by several members of the UEE, and according to the *Gazette*, the new team would 'undoubtedly be a very powerful eleven at all points of the game.' The *Gazette* added that 'the popularity and talent of the whole team, combined with the general esteem their worthy secretary is held in by all classes of cricketers, will ensure them plenty of matches.' So Willsher was still greatly respected by his fellow professionals, but what of their attitude to other cricketers not at this meeting? Why did they feel it necessary to set up a United *South* of England Eleven?

The answer lay in a series of petty disputes between north and south going back to 1859 and typified by 'Willsher's Match' of 1862. The no-balling incident was seen by some of the northern professionals involved as a clandestine plot by the Surrey authorities to save the county from an ignominious defeat, and it led to a decision to boycott matches at The Oval for the foreseeable future. Rumblings of discontent continued until a perceived slight

---

14   Indeed *Wisden* records that Willsher was among the congregation for Lillywhite's funeral at Highgate Cemetery in October 1874.

Overarm at Last

The bread and butter job. The United South of England Eleven, managed by Willsher, which played a local twenty at the Dripping Pan, Lewes, over three days in September 1865. Players only, from left: E.W.Pooley (wk), W.Mortlock, Jas.Lillywhite jun, T.Hearne, John Lillywhite (seated), E.Willsher, J.Caesar, G.Griffith, T.Lockyer, H.Jupp, T.Humphrey (seated). T.Sewell (umpire) is seated in dark jacket.

during their Islington fixture of September 1864 led the South of England team to refuse to play the North at Newmarket in the return match planned for October. This 'north-south' schism was officially confirmed when seven members of the UEE resigned in order to form the new eleven. If they carried on playing for John Wisden's outfit, they would inevitably be forced to play against northerners from time to time, especially in the AEE fixtures, but with their own team they could pick and choose their opponents. Many requests for matches did reach Willsher at his Maidstone home in the winter of 1864/65, and the next summer saw the United South of England Eleven (USEE) engaged in 14 minor matches, in eleven of which Edgar took part. The biggest fixture was the last of the season, against the Gentlemen of Surrey at The Oval. The amateurs were immeasurably strengthened by the addition of W.G.Grace's older brother, E.M., who performed the match double with 120 runs and 13 wickets over the two innings, helping to inflict defeat on the USEE for the fourth time in its inaugural season.

From Willsher's point of view, it was not the first time he had tried to run a travelling team. *Lillywhite's Guide* for 1864 tells us that he, 'with H.H.Stephenson, is manager of the newly established "English Eleven".' Stephenson had been the captain of the first side to tour Australia in 1861/62, and was aware that George Parr's team was not due back from the antipodes until mid-June 1864. As a lot of the squad were from the two main national elevens, he and Willsher decided to plug the early-season gap with a team made up from those left behind in England. The venture was extremely short-lived, with only three fixtures before the Australian touring party returned home, and the 'English Eleven' was never heard of again. The USEE, on the other hand, was a long-term project, and took up a lot of Willsher's time throughout the decade. The culmination of all his hard work came in 1870, when, after the demise of the AEE v UEE match in 1869, a game was organised between the USEE and a 'United North of England Eleven' (UNEE) at Lord's. Although a cricketing flop, with the UNEE winning easily in two days by an innings, it did manage, in the words of the *Times*, 'to heal a long-standing breach among the players'. At last the worst was over, and cricket once again had reason to be very thankful to 'dear old Ned Willsher'.

Perhaps all the extra work involved in running the USEE had some effect on his own form, for in three seasons between 1865 and 1867, Willsher's bowling average was a relatively high 14.38 for 150 first-class wickets.[15] Certainly, Alfred Lubbock, the old Etonian and Kentish amateur, writing in *Wisden* in 1909, felt that he 'slowed down a good deal' after being forced to lower his arm, and he never seems to have regained his former liveliness. In its obituary piece, *Bell's Life* described Willsher as 'medium pace', and the writer must surely have only seen his subject in the later stages of his career, for nowhere else is he downgraded to this extent. There were still some prodigious feats though, both of wicket-taking and economy. Chief among them was his performance for England at the end of July 1866, again against Surrey at The Oval. In a match made famous by the eighteen-year-old W.G. Grace's double of scoring his first first-class hundred (224 not out) and then winning the 440 yards hurdles at Crystal Palace on the same evening, Willsher calmly took seven wickets in the match for just 38 runs off 41 overs, 26 of which were maidens.

Even more outstanding was his bowling for the USEE at Southgate in 1867. Against a decent batting line-up, he started his second innings spell with 13 successive maidens, and at one time he had bowled 27 successive overs for just two runs. W.H.Knight, the

---

15 Wickets cost on average 16.87 over these three seasons.

editor of *Wisden*, was scoring in this match and referred to it in the 1870 issue of the almanack as Willsher's 'most extraordinary bit of bowling of all' and as 'a surprising and marvellous display of truthful bowling.' There was, surely, life in the old dog yet.

Chapter Ten
Captain of England

Happily, Edgar's fortieth year saw no diminution in his powers; quite the contrary. Passing a century of dismissals for the first time, he finished fifth in the first-class averages in the hot, dry summer of 1868 with 113 wickets at 9.98,[16] miserly bowling even by his standards. His strike rate was back down to 35, after hitting 47 in 1867, and his economy rate was a startling 28.[17] For the only time in his career, he completed a hat-trick in top-class cricket, appearing for the Players of the South against the Gentlemen of the South. All three victims were clean bowled, 'a new bat being forthwith presented to him', according to the *Daily News*. Far from putting his feet up, though, the end of the season saw him embark upon an adventure that was to prove more momentous even than that of 1862, and lay any lingering doubts about his reputation permanently to rest.

Yet it could so easily have happened much earlier in his career. In the summer of 1859, George Parr was assembling a squad of professionals for what is now recognised as the first-ever overseas tour, to Canada and the United States in the autumn of that year. As reported by the *New York Commercial Advertiser* in August, Willsher's name was included amongst such heavyweights as Caffyn, Carpenter and Wisden. In the end he had to withdraw, presumably because of the death in September of his first child, John Edgar, at the age of only three months. Edgar senior's interest must have been aroused, because two years later, his name cropped up again as a potential tourist. *Bell's Life* of 1 September 1861 reported that seven players had already signed contracts, and that five more, including Willsher, were expected to follow suit. Again, it was not to be, and Edgar had now also missed out on the first tour of Australia. Finally, George Parr considered him a certainty for his 1863 venture down under, but in the end he was replaced, without explanation, by William Clarke's son Alfred, a

---

16   First-class wickets cost on average 15.07 in this year.
17   In a modern compilation based on the ACS list of first-class matches. He reached 1,000 wickets in first-class cricket in his last match of the 1868 season, though of course this was not something which was recorded or celebrated at the time. He was the sixth bowler (but the first left-armer) to reach this milestone.

Captain of England

Members of the All-England side at Niagara Falls on 20 September 1868. Standing (l to r): unidentified, G.Griffith, unidentified, G,Freeman. Seated: Jas Lillywhite jun, H.Jupp, J.Smith, T.Humphrey. On the ground: A.Shaw, E.Willsher (capt), H.R.J.Charlwood. Three players, Tarrant, Rowbotham and Pooley, were absent from this photograph.

Cricket action at the Garrison ground in St Catherine Street, Montreal in the 1860s. Willsher's eleven scored 310 here in reply to the 28 scored by the local twenty-two.

handy cricketer but clearly not in the same league.

The first inklings the press had of any plans for the off-season of 1868 came at the beginning of August that year. On 1 August, *Harper's Weekly* in New York noted:
> The cricketers of the country are making arrangements for a vigorous season, and the game is growing in favor daily. Among the anticipated sensations is the arrival here of the All-England Eleven – an event in cricketing circles which the St George's Club has been active in endeavoring to secure. It is hoped that this Club will be induced to come here as the guests of the St George's in September or October next, and, if so, they will probably make a tour of the principal Eastern cities and visit Canada.

By 23 August, the *New York Times* was speaking far more emphatically:
> It is now a settled fact that the much-talked-of matches between a selected eleven of the All England Club (Old Country) and the leading associations of this country will take place next month. All preliminary arrangements have been made, and it is expected 'The Eleven' will arrive out the first week in September.

The English press, showing its contempt for the American game, paid the story little attention until the beginning of September. On 5 September, two days after the team had set sail, the identities of both the captain and the organiser of the party were finally revealed:
> Mr V.E.Walker had the task of selecting them, and there could not have been a better man found for the office. Willsher knows as well as anyone how to manage a team, and in addition to this, he is so much, and deservedly, respected by cricketers generally, that under his guidance we have much reasonable hope that all will go 'merry as a marriage bell' with the twelve.

Finally, Edgar was belatedly being given the recognition he deserved – he was captain of an England touring side![18]

Quite how or why Walker became involved, is not clear – both Bettesworth and 'Old Ebor' completely neglect to mention the episode – but from the American point of view it is certain that attempts to secure the trip had been impressively well-organised.

---

18   His first first-class match as captain was for South v North at Rochdale in August 1860.

A committee was formed early in the year from members of the St George's Club of New York, and the Philadelphia, Germantown and Young America Clubs of Philadelphia, and it appears that Willsher had always been the man that they had in mind. Certainly, the combination of recent notoriety and general popularity amongst his fellow professionals made him a marketable choice, and the terms on offer for two months work were appealing to him. Each player was to receive $250 (£50) in gold, plus $7.50 a day and all travel expenses. In addition, they were to take part in several baseball matches in return for a third of the gate money. Not bad recompense for someone in the twilight of his career.

All in all, though, the deal was no more favourable than the $50 plus expenses offered to Parr's pioneers of 1859, as accommodation had to be paid for out of the $7.50 allowance, and returns from novelty baseball matches would be uncertain at best. This may explain the fact that Willsher's twelve, although of good quality, was not fully representative of the cream of English professional cricket. In contrast, the group so colourfully chronicled in Frederick Lillywhite's *The English Cricketers' Trip* was the pick of the AEE and the UEE, with Parr himself, at the peak of his game, joined by legends such as Wisden and Jackson in the bowling department, and batsmen Hayward and Carpenter of Cambridgeshire. The *Montreal Gazette* summed up the general feeling when it opined that 'a stronger eleven, if not two, could be chosen out of the professionals left at home.'

The fact that batsmen of the calibre of Richard Daft, Hayward and Carpenter could not be prevailed upon to make the trip was probably as much to do with the stomach-churning nature of an autumnal Atlantic crossing as anything else. The latter pair, along with all of the rest of the class of '59, would have needed far greater financial incentive to undergo that particular unpleasantness again. Indeed, the only members of the twelve who had experienced a long sea voyage were George Griffith, who went to Australia in 1861/62, and George Tarrant, who toured the same country in 1863/64. The rest of the party would simply have to take their chances.

Another George, Wootton of Nottinghamshire, was notable by his absence, as was the great James Southerton of Surrey and Sussex, who had been the leading wicket-taker in 1868 with 150 at 13.86. Otherwise the bowling was full strength. As well as Willsher, Griffith (although on this tour he bowled mainly slow under-arm lobs) and Tarrant, the pace quartet included Yorkshire's 25-year-old George Freeman, rapidly replacing Tarrant as the fastest and straightest bowler in the land. The attack was completed by Alfred Shaw of Nottinghamshire, who celebrated his 26th birthday on the trip out, and James Lillywhite junior, cousin of Edgar's old friend John and later the England captain in the first-ever Test match in 1877. Both Shaw, medium-pace right-arm, and Lillywhite, slow-medium left-arm, were renowned for their niggardly accuracy, and would make a perfect foil for the more explosive talents of Freeman and Tarrant. As it transpired, the latter was to be called on infrequently throughout the tour, and indeed his powers had finally started to wane; less than two years later he was dead from pleurisy at the age of 31.

The core of the batting was the Surrey opening partnership of Tom Humphrey and Harry Jupp, enthusiastically dubbed the 'Siamese twins' by the *Montreal Gazette*. Humphrey, known as the 'Pocket Hercules' due to his diminutive stature – although not quite the 4 ft 4 in claimed by the *Gazette* – was slightly more dashing than Jupp, who picked up the sobriquet of 'Young Stonewall'. Both had compiled two first-class hundreds during the season just finished, with Jupp the leading scorer with 965 runs at 24.74. After these two, the best of the remainder was Cambridgeshire's John Smith, a

Willsher's men. The All-England Eleven which played six matches in the United States and Canada in September and October 1868.
Standing (l to r): J.Rowbotham, A.Shaw, G.Freeman, E.Willsher (capt), G.F.Tarrant, H.Jupp, E.W.Pooley (wk).
Seated: H.R.J.Charlwood, G.Griffith, J.Smith, Jas.Lillywhite jun, T.Humphrey.

leading light in the AEE and therefore well used to batting against teams of 22 as he would have to throughout his jaunt through North America. The numbers were made up by the youngster of the party, Sussex's Henry Charlwood, a promising but unproven 21-year-old, and the veteran Yorkshireman, roly-poly Joseph Rowbotham, at this stage of his career more useful as a longstop than anything else. Finally, the 'loose cannon' was Surrey's Edward Pooley, a brilliant but personally flawed wicketkeeper. The *Sporting Gazette*, while appreciative of his prowess behind the stumps, sounded a warning note:

> Pooley's dextrous wicket-keeping will earn for him golden opinions from the Yankees, if his usual accompanying foolery does not disgust them.

Overall, it considered the selections very suitable for an arduous trip:

> The list includes two, at least, of the 'fast school' of professionals, but, speaking generally, we have every confidence in the whole of the team that has been sent out, and believe that they will conduct themselves as well socially as they are certain to professionally ... this visit to America will also, we hope, do great things for our home cricket, for the team is made up of several North and South of England young players, who will probably commence a friendship which ought to be thoroughly cemented before their return, and so a good deal more of the horrid cricket schism may perhaps fall away.

At the time of sailing, six matches against odds had been fixed, but more were hoped for; as usual with early cricket tours, the itinerary was necessarily fluid. The plan was to start with a game in New York against the 'United States', before moving to Montreal to play the local garrison and friends. The cricketing circus would then stop in Boston for one match, and return to New York for the grand finale after whetting the appetite with two more games against Philadelphia's finest. There was a possibility that more fixtures would be arranged, but much depended on the results of fund-raising and the interest shown in those games already confirmed. Much encouragement was to be gained from the fact that $4,500 had been pledged in Philadelphia alone, along with $1,000 in Montreal. It had been agreed that half the overall liability was to be met by the St George's Club, with the remainder shared between the Philadelphia clubs, and as their target had been only $3,000 the denizens of the City of Love had every reason to be pleased with themselves.

Edgar too would have been content that the frenetic round of negotiations was finally over and the real business could commence. As he boarded the *S.S. City of Baltimore* at Liverpool on 2 September, he could only hope that the passage would be a lot smoother than that of the *Nova Scotian* nine years before. Certainly, there was no lack of modern technology at the disposal of ship's captain Robert Leitch. Built in 1855 by Tod and McGregor of Glasgow for the Inman Line, *City of Baltimore* was a three-masted, iron-hulled, single-screw steamship weighing in at 2,368 tons, with a top speed of 10 knots. Initially she was chartered by the French in the Crimean war, before starting her first commercial journeys between Liverpool and Philadelphia in 1856. In 1866 she was reconditioned with new engines and boilers and resumed passages to New York, now via Queenstown in County Cork. However, all this meant nothing if the Atlantic threw up any of the 'equinoctial gales' that plagued the 1859 trip, described at comic length by Fred Lillywhite.

Willsher's side made their transatlantic crossing on the S.S. City of Baltimore, of a modest 2,400 tons, here seen taking on oceanic weather.

Fred's brother John, along with Alfred Clarke, was there to see off the intrepid travellers, and he would have had a particular professional interest in doing so, as his *Companion* was the only publication, apart from some of the newspapers, to give the tour any coverage. Presumably cousin James was deputed to provide the account that eventually appeared in the 1869 edition, as he was later to collaborate in the production of the family annual, and he may well also have been the 'correspondent' who provided regular updates for the readers of *Bell's Life*.

On 3 September, the only stop of the trip was made in Queenstown (Cobh) in County Cork, to pick up its cargo of Irish emigrants, the majority of whom would be paying $30 for steerage in the hope of finding their fortune in the New World. As for the rest of the journey, 'it was not all sweets' according to James Lillywhite, and indeed the seasickness of the first few days was such that 'several wished they had never ventured'. George Freeman, in a letter home to his wife, confirmed that most, but not all, of the twelve were bad sailors:

> ... the four or five first days were ones of sorrow for most of us, and we wished many times that we were back in dear old England. We were all bad with sea-sickness, except Rowbotham, Willsher and Griffith, and it was a great treat to hear us all kicking up the most horrible rows imaginable. ... Four of us slept in one berth, and it was just like lying on the shelves in the pantry at home. ... We have on board about 950 souls, with the crew. One death took place and we had also a birth, so that in all we finished as we started.

Alfred Shaw was particularly impressed by the considerable intestinal fortitude of those left standing:

> Joe Rowbotham ... received the name of 'Old Tar Pot' on this journey. The reason was that on board ship he stuck to everything he had to eat, in contrast to most of the members of the party, who missed more meals and paid more painful visits to the ship's side than can be recorded. George Griffith and Rowbotham never missed a meal between Liverpool and New York. For a few days they had our party's table to themselves, and their excellent appetites were reflected in their sleek forms and rubicund faces. When the bad sailors had sufficiently recovered to face the dinner table and claim their own share of the fare, Rowbotham and Griffith complained that they could not get enough to eat!

Perhaps the period mentioned by Freeman and Lillywhite coincided with the four days of fog described by Shaw, ending in a near miss with an iceberg. However, after a week of relative calm in which to recover their health and spirits, the team were greeted on the morning of Sunday, 13 September, by a magnificent view of the Hudson River as the ship slowly steamed into New York harbour. On their arrival at two o'clock a letter was handed to Willsher, inviting the whole party to stay for free at Mr W.B.Burrows' Everett

House Hotel in Union Square. After eleven long days at sea, nobody needed to be asked twice.

The Everett House was a hotel built in the grandest style in 1848, and was the Prince of Wales' hostelry of choice when, in 1860, his mother, Queen Victoria, sent him on a goodwill mission to the American colonies at the tender age of 18. It was certainly well situated, being right in the heart of New York's commercial district, at the intersection of Broadway and Bowery Road (now Fourth Avenue), and with several horse-drawn tram lines running through it. The centrepiece of the Square was a bronze statue of George Washington on horseback, erected in 1856. It was so fashionable by 1870 that Tiffany's moved their premises there from Broadway, and an indicator of its political significance was its use as the site of the first Labor Day parade in 1882.

If Edgar's men had fallen on their feet, British and Irish immigrants would undoubtedly not have been so lucky. New York was by now a bustling metropolis of just over a million souls, many of whom were inevitably exposed to the extremes that any big city had to offer. In his book *The Secrets of the Great City*, published in the same year, Edward Winslow Martin described this very modern problem:

> Strangers coming to New York are struck with the fact that there are but two classes in the city – the poor and the rich. The middle class, which is so numerous in other cities, hardly exists at all here ... leave Broadway opposite the New York Hospital, and pass down Pearl Street in an easterly direction. Five minutes walking will bring you to the abode of poverty and suffering, a locality which contrasts strangely with the elegant thoroughfare we have just left ... in a few minutes you will see that blessed beacon of light in this great sea of human misery and sin, the 'Five Points Mission.' You are now fairly in the heart of the Five Points district. It is a horrible place, and you shudder as you look at it. The streets are dark and narrow, the dwellings are foul and gloomy, and seem filled with mystery and crime.

We can be sure that the England party, only too familiar with such sights in all the major cities back home, were kept strictly on the tourist trail for the duration of their trip. They were, after all, here to play cricket, not change the world.

Just three years after the end of the Civil War – an event handily summarised by Ben Stiller in *Night at the Museum* as 'North wins; slavery is bad' – cricket in America was in dire need of a boost.

After a sluggish start in the first third of the century, the game began to take root with increasing urbanisation, as evidenced by the formation of the St George's Cricket Club in 1840, and New York CC in 1844. No longer was it considered a pastime only suitable for children, and it became organised to the extent that St George's was employing no less than six professionals by 1848. The press began to show an interest, and the public flocked in their thousands to games such as the world's first international contest, against Canada at Hoboken, New Jersey, in 1844. The ground at Hoboken, known as the Elysian Fields, is also claimed by its supporters as the venue of the first organised baseball match in America in 1846. Thereafter, it was a fight to the death between the two major bat-and-ball sports, and the Civil War left cricket bloodied if, for the moment, unbowed.

There had always been a suggestion that cricket was a snobbish occupation, especially in the hands of the St George's Club, whose members tended to be exclusively English, and therefore, at least in the view of some of the press, resistant to the spread of the game amongst native-born Americans. The idea that cricket was failing to thrive because of nationalistic sentiments was fuelled by newspapers like the *New York Clipper*, which also highlighted the difference in pace of the two games:

> now-a-days, with the popular National Game to contend against, very few can be induced to witness a game which takes as many days to decide as it does hours to play a game of base ball.

On the face of it, this might give hope to those seeking to market Twenty20 as a viable format in the USA, but, in truth, it is increasingly clear at this distance in time that cricket could never supplant baseball in the national psyche because its structure was already well-established when it arrived on American shores, whereas baseball was still at an embryonic stage, and therefore ripe for change through trial and error. Thus, it became a game that not only suited the American attention span, but also, in the words of the *New York Times*, promoted 'the manly attributes of pluck, courage, endurance, activity and judgment.'

Despite the onward march of baseball, the St George's Club was determined to keep its end up, and, having lost its lease on the Elysian Fields and failed to secure a pitch in Central Park itself, it set about finding new headquarters. On 20 April 1867, the *Clipper* announced:

> This Club recently effected the purchase of a new ground

on Bergen Hill at a cost of over $35,000, which, with the pavilion to be erected thereon, is expected to be in readiness to play by the middle of next month, and will probably be unexcelled in regard to size, location, and appointments, by any cricket or ball field in the world.

Today, no reminders are left of the complex, situated in the densely populated district of Bergenwood about two miles northwest of the Elysian Fields, but the contemporary Grove Church Cemetery still lies opposite what would have been the entrance, on the corner of Bergenwood Avenue and 46th Street. As it happened, the timescale predicted proved to be a trifle optimistic, but nevertheless the first game at the new ground was finally played on 8 July 1868 between St George's and Philadelphia's Young America Club. A week later, a combined St George's and Philadelphia team met the Knickerbocker Club of Montreal and secured a crushing victory by ten wickets. New York was as ready as it could be for its distinguished visitors – whether St George's could live up to their billing as 'Dragon Slayers' remained to be seen.

First, however, the tourists needed to acclimatise and be pampered by their hosts. On Monday, 14 September, the St George's club laid on a coach and four to take the English on the three-mile journey to the new ground. A pleasant afternoon was spent surveying the scene, in the centre of which 'sixty yards square ... is perfectly level and the herbage green ... with a little attention a very nice wicket can be got ready.' After a week of warm sunshine, rain arrived, limiting the twelve's practice to half an hour, and, since Tuesday, the last day before the game, was reserved for watching a baseball match, that would have to do. After a photo opportunity the next morning, it was off to the Union Base Ball Ground in Brooklyn to watch the Union Club entertaining the Mutual. The ground was notable for being one of the first to be fully enclosed, and on the day the crowd of 5,000 inside was considerably swollen, in the words of the *Brooklyn Daily Eagle*, by 'fence-protectors and curbstone recliners'. The English visitors, after a brief practice with some of the players, were invited into the three-storey pagoda that stood rather incongruously in the centre of the outfield, and with the Union Jack fluttering happily above them, they watched the home team complete a resounding victory.

The day of the match, Wednesday, 16 September, dawned cold and windy with a hint of rain in the air, and no doubt the threatening aspect of the weather deterred many from venturing to Hudson

City for the tour's opening salvoes. About 1,200 attended, well short of capacity, and most of them preferred to stand rather than pay the unannounced charge for seating – a further dent to the St George's Club's already tarnished image. According to an unreferenced report from the Philadelphia Cricket Club scrapbook:

> About one hundred of these were women. There were half a dozen buxom English girls with fine, fresh faces and magnificent heads of hair, and the remaining females were those who had come to America early in life and were since domiciled but not naturalized in this country. Of the men, perhaps three-fourths were English-born and had English manners and ways about them.

As it turned out, the 'United States' team initially promised had become 'Twenty-Two of New York', and even that was made up of players from only three clubs. Naturally, St George's dominated with 14 members, the remainder of the team coming equally from the New York and Willow clubs. Names to watch out for included former Kent fast bowler Fred Norley, and the brothers Harry and George Wright. The Wright family had emigrated from Sheffield to New York in 1836, and by 1857 Harry, then aged 22, was earning $12 a week as a professional at St George's. Both he and George played in international matches against Canada, but talents such as theirs were inevitably poached by baseball. By the time of Willsher's visit, they were regarded as the finest exponents

Harry Wright, English-born professional at the St George's Cricket Club in New York, pictured with his father, Sam (at left) in 1864. Harry later turned to baseball.

of the national sport in the whole country, so their appearance on the cricket field was both a considerable drawcard and an endorsement of the continuing appeal of the more venerable game. It also appeased their father Sam, himself a professional at St George's, who was no doubt disappointed by their preference for America's new-fangled pastime.

Round about noon, Willsher successfully carried out his most important task as captain by winning the toss and deciding to make first use of a pitch described by the *Brooklyn Eagle* as 'not as good as it might have been.' At 12.20 pm, to the accompanying 'smell of chowder ... with the slight odour of onions mixed', Humphrey and Jupp finally walked out to face the opening attack of Norley and Harry Wright, a handy combination when backed up by twenty outfielders. Norley bowled the first ball of the tour to Humphrey, which he successfully 'blockaded', and he saw off the rest of the over without mishap. Jupp recorded the first run in the next over when he turned Wright to leg for two, and matters proceeded quietly until the sixth over, when Norley dropped Humphrey at slip off Wright. The reprieve was short lived, however, as in Wright's next over, Humphrey was bowled for five 'by a splendid ball, which merited the applause so liberally bestowed.' Nine for one.

Next in was Smith, who steadied any residual nerves in a calm and confident stand with Jupp, treating the crowd to 'an exhibition of well-defended wickets. The batting was not only scientific but powerful, and great prudence and judgment was shown in the cuttings, blockings, and drivings.' By such methods, they had advanced the score to 30 before Wright made way for the gentler pace of Butterfield, who toiled to little effect. Finally, the persevering Norley induced Smith to play on with the total at 45, his own contribution to a partnership of 36 being a classy 22, including the first boundary of the match, awarded three runs under local regulations. Lillywhite then joined Jupp to take proceedings up to lunch, which, in traditional, and no doubt liquid, fashion, lasted well over an hour. Not long after the interval, Lillywhite fell with the score at 71, bringing in Shaw to accompany the 'Pocket Stonewall' for a further half hour of dour defence. At last, Jupp, 'who, to all appearance, had made up his mind to stay till dark', was bowled by Norley to make it 79 for four. He had held the bowling at bay for over two hours for his 23.

After Jupp's demise, a mid-innings 'wobble' was threatened when Norley had Tarrant lbw for a duck, but Pooley's arrival heralded a more positive approach as the shadows lengthened. By the close, he had reached 18 and Freeman three out of 126 for seven. Shaw and Rowbotham had both played their part in stabilising the innings with solid double-figure contributions. Although their batting had hardly set the world alight, England had made a fair start against some keen fielding, and only after the Americans' first innings reply would they discover whether they had made a par score.

When play resumed at 11.30 the next day, more than 3,000 spectators had gathered, including many more of the 'fair sex'. Norley swiftly disposed of Pooley and Freeman, leaving England precariously placed at 139 for nine. Willsher then demonstrated that he was no ordinary number eleven by making a lively contribution to a last-wicket stand of 36, and, by the time he was caught in the outfield for 16, the total had climbed to a respectable 175. Norley had toiled manfully for 80 four-ball overs, 43 of them maidens, and had finished with the deserved figures of six for 67. In all, the innings had lasted 159.3 overs, giving an excruciating scoring rate of 27 runs per 100 balls.

If England could claim that fast scoring was impossible with the outfield so densely populated, the Americans had no such excuse for their even more sluggish 26 per 100 balls. They were simply outclassed. Willsher and Freeman bowled unchanged through 58.3 overs as the pick of New York was bundled out for just 61. They were brilliantly supported in the field, Rowbotham being especially outstanding at longstop, where he let only four balls past him all innings. Willsher picked up 13 wickets for 23 and Freeman seven for 28, with Norley being run out. Following on at 5.15 that night, the Americans closed at 10 for three, and the organisers were already planning an exhibition match the next day in case of an early finish.

They need not have worried. The New Yorkers rallied to such an extent that at one stage, with the score 56 for 10, it was hoped that they could hang on for a draw, but once Rogerson, elevated to number four after being last man in the first innings, had gone for 22, the remainder of the batting fell away. At four o'clock, the last wicket fell at 88, leaving England worthy victors by an innings and 26 runs. Indeed, most of the interest had gone out of the match by stumps on the second day, and, as if aware of this, the fielding was not up to the exalted standards of the first innings. Willsher had given himself a deserved rest, leaving the field clear for Alfred Shaw, who captured nine for 21 in 25 overs.

The entertainment did not stop there though. Harry Wright picked eight of the eleven to be on his side in an impromptu baseball match against a team cobbled together from five of the St George's Club and various waifs and strays, 'decided muffins' according to the *New York Times*. Failing light limited play to five innings, but the English had plenty of time to show their prowess in the new-fangled sport. Rowbotham proved an able pitcher, and with the fielding rediscovering its usual sharpness, Wright's team ran out easy winners by 39 to 14. Next time the hosts would have to take the event rather more seriously. Indeed, three days later, the following advertisement appeared in the *Brooklyn Eagle*:

> TO THE ALL ENGLAND ELEVEN ... We do hereby challenge you to play the Atlantic nine a game of base ball ... An early reply would ... set to rest the many rumors that are talked about among the base ball public concerning your purpose to play the game. If this challenge is accepted the game will be one of the sensations of the season.

The Atlantics were the top side in the country in 1868, and so such a match would truly decide who were the superior ball players in the eyes of all right-thinking Americans.

The Brooklyn Atlantics baseball side of 1869.
The club issued a public challenge in 1868 to Willsher's side to play baseball, but nothing came of it.

At this juncture, the tourists were en route to Montreal, with the more serious business of cricket on their minds. They could reflect on a job professionally done, and the authorities could be satisfied that the first leg of the trip had been a success, both financially and in the promotion of the rival summer game. Only the *New York Clipper* offered a dissenting voice, concluding scathingly:

> With the single exception of a hungry representative of the fourth estate, who is always about when there is anything to eat, and who generally toadies to anybody and everything that will afford him a chance for a 'free lunch', the efforts of the club to have the 'great match' written up so as to attract a multitude was a signal failure.

There was no doubt cricket was becoming increasingly hard to sell to native-born Americans, and publicity like this did not help. However, the more discerning reader was well aware that such invective could be treated with a pinch of salt – the *Clipper* and the St George's Club were destined never to see eye to eye.

Chapter Eleven
Cricket on the Brain

> 'Cricket' is the talk in this city at the present time. For some weeks past Cricket has engrossed the public attention, and now that the grand contest is going on, everybody seems to be seized with 'Cricket on the brain'.

So wrote 'Alpha' in a letter sent from Montreal to the readers of the *Boston Evening Transcript*. He goes on to describe a city 'laden with crowds of pleasure tourists', reflecting the new-found confidence in the country after the passing of the British North America Act had created the Dominion of Canada only a year previously. Yet ties with the Mother Country could not be so easily broken; soon after becoming Canada's first Prime Minister, Sir John Macdonald declared cricket the national sport. Indeed, the 'Twenty-Two of Canada' arrayed in front of Willsher's men consisted of a mixture of Canadian civilians and British soldiers from the Montreal garrison. Despite its French origins, Montreal was now, with a population of at least 100,000, the largest city in British North America and the economic and cultural heart of Canada. However, cricket's grip on the public imagination was to be short-lived. Although there was no showcase baseball match on this trip, as cultural exchanges with the United States expanded in the 1870s inevitably the quintessential American sport rapidly replaced cricket as the nation's favourite pastime.

For the moment, the tyranny of distance somewhat restricted the march of progress, as Ned and team discovered on their three-day trudge from New York to Montreal. After taking in the delights of Niagara Falls on Sunday, 20 September, they finally reached their destination at 10 o'clock on Monday night, having changed trains no fewer than three times. Once again, they were treated to top-class accommodation at the St Lawrence Hall, another of the Prince of Wales' favourite haunts in the centre of the city. Unlike in New York, however, the tight schedule meant there was no time for acclimatisation: the match would start the next day. There was just time for Alfred Shaw to record another food-related incident from his time at the St Lawrence:

> At Montreal, where black waiters attended our table,

> Rowbotham ordered chops one morning for breakfast. Three were brought in on a dish. Joe eyed them critically, and then, calling a woolly-headed attendant, astonished him by quietly remarking, 'Tak' these back, and bring us sommat to ate'.

Quite apart from the random racism characteristic of the times, the scenario presented is not one recognisable from the 'supersized' North America of today!

The Garrison ground in St Catherine Street was the hub of cricket in the city until early in the nineteenth century, when rapid commercial development swept it away. However, the church of St James the Apostle, seen in the background in many contemporary images of the ground, is still active today. The city-centre location reflected the importance attached to cricket as a way of keeping up morale both for the military and the locals, and confidence was high after the Garrison team had engineered a four-wicket win over the St George's Club in New York back in July. According to the *Spirit of the Times*, even the English were concerned by the apparent strength of the twenty-two:

> As much loud trumpeting had been done regarding this Montreal match, some little trepidation was felt by the Eleven for their success against them. ... With such a prelude, everybody looked for a contest bordering on the tragical. The result proved the affair ridiculously farcical.

As this correspondent implies, Edgar need not have worried. Indeed, it is best for those of a nervous disposition that they look away briefly as the bare facts of the match are recorded. The Canadians, winning the toss and making first use of a rain-deadened wicket, were rolled over in two hours for 28, Willsher and Freeman bowling straight through. In all, sixteen ducks were registered, and only Rose, with 12, reached double figures. Freeman had 13 wickets for 12, and Willsher eight for 13. By the close on the first day, the eleven was already well in the lead with 47 for one. Sandwiched between two complete washouts on days two and four, the English did pretty much what they liked with the bowling, racking up 310 all out by the close of the third day. Griffith made particularly merry with 69, which turned out to be the highest innings of the whole tour. Although the match was left technically as a draw, all concerned regarded it as a moral victory. Despite the feebleness of the opposition and the dismal weather, the two days possible had attracted an overall crowd of about 5,000, so at least the organisers could be pleased with the return on their $1,000.

A much sterner test awaited in Boston, which the party reached at nine o'clock on Saturday after a pleasant overnight trip. The gentle nature of the hospitality on the whole trip was reinforced by a visit that afternoon to the city of Cambridge to see the universities of Harvard and Brown playing baseball, where, although clearly following carefully, the visitors displayed their ignorance through asking questions, according to the *Boston Herald*, that 'showed plainly that they had still a very imperfect idea of the rules.' Any chance of having a sneak preview of the wicket for Monday's match was ruined by a torrential downpour on the Sunday, which was spent attending church and listening to an organ recital at the city's Music Hall, concluded diplomatically by the playing of the two countries' national anthems. In Boston, as in all other cities visited, there is no record of the banqueting and speech-making so prevalent on tours of the time, no doubt much to the relief of the England captain, who, although generous to a fault and universally popular, would probably have been a reluctant speech-maker and keen to avoid the limelight.

Riverside Park, venue for a further three-day game against a twenty-two made up of 16 local players supplemented by the likes of George Wright and Norley from St George's, and two of Philadelphia's Newhall brothers, was actually a 'trotting', or harness-racing, racecourse situated in Allston, about three miles from the middle of Boston. Opened in 1865, it was the scene of a world record when 'Captain McGowan' trotted no less than 20 miles in just 56 minutes and 25 seconds, netting its owner a purse of $5,500. Little wonder that the cricket pitch, prepared at little more than a month's notice, was by far the worst experienced on tour.

Draper, Boston's captain, won the toss and decided, given the state of the wicket, to insert the Englishmen. The ground was not dry enough to start until 2.30, and when play did finally commence, Humphrey and Jupp were even more cautious than usual. They were up against probably America's finest opening pair in Norley and Charles Newhall (of whom more later) and had scratched about for three in eight overs when Newhall removed Humphrey, caught at slip. Despite the late start, in time-honoured fashion lunch was taken after just forty-five minutes of play, with England 20 for one. On the resumption, John Smith dominated the scoring to the extent that, when Jupp was bowled by Norley for three, the total had already advanced to 30. Smith was soon out himself for 26 out of a total of 33, and the rest of day was dominated by Griffith, who continued where he had left off in Canada. By the close, he was 41 not out, but he had lost Freeman and Rowbotham cheaply on the way to 80 for five. It had been the hardest day yet, but at least humiliation had been avoided.

If the bowling was far more taxing than anything faced in Canada, the home team's batting was little better. After the eleven's innings had closed on the second morning at 109 (Griffith 48 and Pooley 17), the twenty-two caved in under the sustained pressure, once again, of Willsher and Freeman. Wright top-scored with 12 in a total of just 39, Freeman again taking the lion's share of the wickets with 13 for 16, Willsher supporting brilliantly with seven for 15. Wickets continued to tumble in England's second innings, only Jupp holding his end up for long, remaining 17 not out at the end of the day out of a disappointing 33 for four.

Play resumed on the Wednesday in front of a crowd much reduced from the 5,000 of the day before, and although England were easily got out for 71 in the morning (Jupp 36) the home team did nothing in their second innings to suggest that those who stayed away had made the wrong decision. Willsher again stepped aside to allow Tarrant some exercise, and he took full advantage with 12 for 16. Freeman continued his wicketfest with seven for 14. The only consolation in a defeat by 104 runs was the fact that they had managed to keep the eleven in the field until four o'clock on the final afternoon.

After taking a bow in full cricket costume on stage at the Theatre Comique on Wednesday night, the tourists returned to Riverside Park the next morning for a baseball match against three of the local clubs. Ned sat this one out, along with Freeman, Lillywhite and Griffith. George Wright stood in as pitcher for the Englishmen, and attracted most of the plaudits from the local press. After a defeat by 21 to 4, it was felt only fair that in future matches the full eleven should be allowed to play. In those circumstances, their keen fielding might pull them through, despite their ignorance of the 'finer points' of the game. Finally, the colonial upstarts had something to teach their former masters!

With no time to lose, the twelve took the 5.45 pm train to New London, arriving there at 10.15 pm, in time for the overnight steamboat to New York. After a sleepless night amidst the hustle and bustle on board ship, the team transferred to the Philadelphia train, reaching their final destination at 4 o'clock in the afternoon of 2 October. This time, there was no delegation to greet the

Cricket on the Brain

Home base at a time of election fever. The Merchant's Hotel in Philadelphia at the time Willsher's team stayed there.

The ground at Nicetown in its early twentieth-century heyday. Willsher's side played two matches here, against odds, in October 1868.

exhausted travellers, and they took their chances as best they could with local accommodation, eventually securing berths at the Merchant's Hotel on Fourth Street. Constructed in 1837 on the original site of the University of Pennsylvania, the Merchant's was renowned for its pioneering use of speaking tubes instead of the sonorous gongs used to summon guests at the remainder of the city's hostelries. Given the trying and tedious nature of the English party's trip to Philadelphia, such a provision was a true act of compassion!

Part of the difficulty in finding quarters was the election fever that was gripping the whole of Pennsylvania. Willsher's men rode into town with only a month to go before the first national vote since the end of the Civil War in 1865, and even at this late stage the outcome was in doubt. Andrew Johnson, who had succeeded Abraham Lincoln as President after the latter's assassination in April 1865, was unable to secure the Democratic nomination for a further term, so it was Horatio Seymour that entered the fray against the Republican's populist choice of war hero Ulysses S.Grant. The main issue at stake was the matter of what became known as 'Reconstruction', the essential difference between the two parties being that Johnson wanted peaceful reconciliation with the South, while Grant was in the hands of the 'Radical Republicans', who urged a more punitive approach. This seems at odds with Grant's campaign slogan of 'let us have peace', but more characteristic of the electioneering was a concerted assault on Seymour's character of which modern spin-doctors would be proud. As it transpired, the result in Pennsylvania was fairly representative of that across the country, with Grant securing 52.2 per cent of the popular vote. Despite an embarrassing loss in New York, at the age of 46 Grant became the youngest United States president at that time, and remained popular enough to be re-elected for a second term in 1872.

Against this background, it is unsurprising that Willsher's tour had a low-key feel to it, even in the cricketing heartland of Philadelphia. Yet there was undoubtedly more interest in the tour than there had been in baseball-hungry New York. A lot of the credit for this had its origins in the 'apple barrage' of 1855, when younger members of the Wister and Newhall families, disgruntled at being excluded because of their tender years from a Germantown Cricket Club match being played on the Wister estate, interrupted play by pelting their elders with apples from the family orchard. The incident came to the attention of Thomas A.Newhall, known as Philadelphia's sugar king, who invited his clan to play on his own estate, along with the six sons of William Wister, another leading local businessman. The resultant Young America Cricket Club not only kept cricket going during the Civil War when adult players were away on active service, but also nurtured an atmosphere in which new, locally born players were actively encouraged in order to promote the game for the future. Above all, although the young gentlemen had picked up the game from Nottingham weavers settled in the Germantown area of Philadelphia, they took it and turned it into the preserve of the native-born upper classes, thus creating a model that could be sustained in the face of outside pressures. Indeed, according to J.Thomas Jable, by 1870 only about one per cent of members of the four major local clubs were born in the United Kingdom, while eight per cent were white-collar workers. Thus, in stark contrast to New York, a small number of Americans had established a climate in which social standing could be enhanced, rather than diminished, by membership of a cricket club.

By 1868, the local scene was very much dominated by the Newhall family. Of the ten brothers, no fewer than seven played for the Young America Club, and there were four in the twenty-two amateurs selected to play in the match beginning the day after the visitors' arrival. The captain, at 23 the oldest sibling on show, was George, described in these terms by the *North American and U.S. Gazette*:

> No-one but those who know would take the pale, quiet looking gentleman ... to be the famous cricketer he is. Should he grasp your hand, however, or place you on the field, you would at once acknowledge that he was more than he looked.

Charles, who had already shown his mettle in Boston, was eulogised as 'the fastest bowler in America, if not in the world'; Daniel, a batting allrounder, was 'the first cricketer in America'; and Robert, only 16, 'the "spider", stands a little bit higher than the wickets.' Overall, Young America was represented by eight players, as was the Philadelphia Club. The remainder of the squad was made up of five from Gentleman, and one I Zingari member. The fledgling Merion Club, founded only in 1865, was not called upon. Nevertheless, the *Gazette* was happy with the selections, promising that 'with ordinary skill and nerve we can beat them; if not, we have the players to give them a tight game.'

Philadelphia was to be all work and no play for Willsher and his charges, as the match commenced the day after their arrival in the city. They were allowed to rest until 11 o'clock, when they were taken by a coach and four to the Germantown Club ground at Nicetown, eight miles from the city centre. Later the site of the Nicetown freight station, the ground is now covered over by industrial units to the south of the Roosevelt Expressway, the legendary route No.1. By the time the coaches drew up at the ground, trainloads of spectators had paid their 50 cents admission and settled in to await their distinguished international guests. The Club's new headquarters had been paid for by Thomas Pratt McKean, son of the second Governor of Pennsylvania, and had reached an immaculate standard, as described by the *Philadelphia Inquirer*:

> The field presented a beautiful appearance, the pavilion of the club affording ample accommodation ... the ground itself was in admirable condition, having been thoroughly drained and resodded early in the spring.

Writing many years later, George Newhall himself gave some indication of the special atmosphere at such international matches:

> The English element would congregate on the 'township line' side of the field to loyally encourage and shout for their visiting countrymen, and the natives, around the ropes, would offset the British enthusiasm and be ever ready to cheer on the Americans; and the 'grandstand', that wonderful assemblage of fair women and brave men (such a picture and such a flutter!), would sympathize with the fallen in a most heartrending way, and laud the heroes to the echo.

Not quite the Barmy Army, but noisy enough with 5,000 present on most days and the Germania Band striking up at regular intervals!

After winning the toss, George Newhall finally marched to the wicket at 1.40 pm accompanied by Charles Cadwalader, a leading member of the organising committee behind the week's entertainment. Freeman gave the English a dream start by bowling Newhall first ball, and he also removed Hargraves in similar fashion with the score at 18. At this point, after an hour's action, a late lunch was taken, which only played into the fielding side's hands. After putting his feet up for an hour, Freeman was able to carry on much as he had all tour, and with Shaw and Tarrant alternating from the other end, he bowled straight through to the close, at which point he had taken 10 for 19 from 26 overs. Only the cautious Cadwalader, with 15 in two hours, looked like offering serious resistance, and the twenty-two would have been glad of an early close at five o'clock, with the scoreboard reading 55 for 13. Willsher was happy to take a back seat and direct operations in the field. Little did he know how vital his allround abilities were to prove as the match wore on.

Play started at the more usual time of 11.30 am after the Sunday rest day, with the sun shining weakly to reflect the fragile state of the local batting. Wickets continued to fall at regular intervals, but at 61 for 16 a little backbone was added by White and Clay, who added 22 in half an hour. Their contributions were crucial in lifting the total to equal that of the New York twenty-two's second innings, 88. When the innings closed at 12.30, Freeman had laboured for 41.3 overs for his analysis of 14 for 15. Tarrant offered sterling support with four for 39, and Lillywhite proved his worth by ending the crucial partnership and finishing with figures of two for 6. There was no reason to suppose that any of the main protagonists would be required to do more than turn their arms over a second time around.

With Humphrey resting and therefore on umpiring duties, John Smith was sent in to open with Jupp against a fielding side that, according to the *New York Herald*, 'in white flannel shirts and knickerbocker breeches and crimson stockings was very picturesque as they were scattered over the dark green sward, which was as level as a billiard table.' Jupp certainly couldn't find a way through them, and was bowled for a duck by Charles Newhall, who proceeded to remove Griffith and Smith to leave the score 7 for three. Spencer Meade of the Philadelphia Cricket Club, 'a fine left-arm bowler with an awful work', then removed Pooley for no score, with England reeling at 11 for four. The crowd, sensing a serious upset, 'went wild', but was silenced by a more sober passage of play in which Shaw and the boy Charlwood inched towards respectability. However, once Shaw was castled by Newhall (35 for five), the procession continued with Lillywhite and Rowbotham failing to trouble the scorers. When lunch was called at two o'clock, the eleven were in a sorry state at 43 for seven. Only Charlwood, unbeaten with a calmly compiled 25, stood between England and a rare humiliation.

After 45 minutes of replenishment, England briefly altered their tactics, and with the aggressive Tarrant at the helm, threw caution to the wind. In a breezy fifteen-minute stand, they put on 22, including a drive by Charlwood over the fence near the pavilion for a welcome six. Gus Waterman then lived up to his reputation as a useful change bowler with 'a peculiar low delivery' by removing both Tarrant and Freeman within the space of three balls, leaving the contest on a knife-edge at 65 for nine. Willsher now played one of the most vital innings of his life, eking out the runs in a watchful partnership punctuated by lusty blows for two and three. Both batsmen were given a chance in the deep, but eventually Charlwood fell caught in the outfield going for another boundary, but not before he had contributed 45 to a total of 92, giving a tiny but precious lead of four runs. His captain remained 13 not out. The *Gazette* reported breathlessly that 'the wonder and astonishment of the spectators was only equalled by the gratification felt by the twenty-two themselves', and certainly the eleven had been rattled by the consistent pace of Charles Newhall, who finished with six for 48.

The fightback began almost as soon as England took the field, but it came not from the expected source of George Freeman, but from Griffith, bowling deceptive 'slow left-hand twisters' that lured unsuspecting batsmen to their fate. By the close he had taken five of the 10 wickets to fall for a dismal 21 runs, and although he had no more success on the resumption, his captain's gamble had paid off. When battle re-commenced the next day, Freeman completed the job in clinical fashion with freakish figures of 13 for 11, including a sensational over containing four wickets in consecutive balls, assisted by Willsher, who picked up a couple of wickets during a spell of nine consecutive maidens. In an all-out total of 35, Hargraves had top-scored with 13, with nobody else managing more than five. The *Gazette* was considerably less jaunty in its appraisal of the Philadelphians' performance: 'Of the batting in this innings ... nothing can be said in commendation ... to say it was poor is about all that is necessary. ... It was a sort of race to see who could stay in the shortest time.' Weekend cricketers around the globe will know the feeling only too well.

With only 32 needed in just over two hours, England's task seemed a formality, but nothing in this match went exactly according to the form-book. After a steady start from Smith and Jupp, the first wicket did not fall until 12 had been compiled in 11 overs, but then the floodgates were opened. Charles Newhall and Meade worked their way steadily through the top order to leave the eleven on the brink at 22 for six. At this point Freeman received a taste of his own medicine, being bowled by Newhall for his second 'blob' of the match: 26 for seven. With Lillywhite at the other end, Griffith continued to chip away calmly at the victory target until, with the scores tied, an incident occurred that provoked scenes reminiscent of The Oval in 1862. Lillywhite himself provides the

following eye-witness account:
> Lillywhite played a ball to the off, and Griffith of course called him and got well home, when an appeal was made and the umpire gave Griffith out, very much to the surprise of all present. This was the means of stopping the match for a time, and the Eleven had very justly to object to the umpire. Never could a more one-sided decision be given, and it was a matter of surprise that an appeal should be made in such a case as the present, but it was quite evident that the Young Americans meant winning, and no matter how ... .

Strong words, fortunately published nearly three weeks after the event. The protest from the batting side was so vociferous that umpire Pepper, himself a replacement for the original official who had given a similarly dodgy decision reprieving a Philadelphian batsman, was removed in favour of Pearson, the Philadelphia Club professional. Naturally enough, the local press was less inclined to criticise what they saw as well-intentioned decisions. The correspondent of the *Inquirer* was of the opinion that 'if the umpire's decisions are to be questioned, and the umpire grossly insulted, as was the case yesterday, the sooner the public know of it the better, as in that case they can withhold their patronage'.

Whatever the rights or wrongs of the matter, Griffith had to go, and all results were still possible at 31 for eight. Pooley, held back by Willsher, now came in to face Meade, and as ever caused 'considerable amusement by his antics about the "popping-crease"', having cut the last ball of the over for what he hoped would be the winning run. Newhall now diplomatically bowled his only wide of the match, and Ned could breathe a double sigh of relief – not only had his team scraped home by two wickets, but he had not been called on to bat in unimaginably tense circumstances. Despite defeat, the hero of the hour was Charles Newhall, with five more wickets for 21, although Freeman, whose 27 wickets were the real difference between the sides, was handed the accolade of 'best bowler that ever trod foot on an American cricket-field'. Perhaps the English had under-estimated their opponents, but the reality was that odds of two to one were always going to be weighted against them on what turned out to be a sluggish playing surface. They would have to be at their best when they re-convened two days later against a team billed portentously as the 'United States'.

The closest match of the tour should perhaps not be left behind without touching upon an interesting sidelight provided by the memoirs of Alfred Shaw. In them he refers to a bet made on board the *City of Baltimore* between Lillywhite and Freeman as to which would be the highest scorer in the New York match. As with all good semi-apocryphal stories, Shaw claims that they both obtained a 'pair of spectacles', whereas in reality, in their *only* innings, Lillywhite scored 13 and Freeman 10. He then conflates the Montreal and Boston matches, again asserting that neither had yet got off the mark on the tour. So to Philadelphia and the final attempt to settle the bet. This is where we have to assume some factual basis to Shaw's account, provided we change some of the names. Both Freeman and Lillywhite had failed to score in the first innings, and Freeman, batting above Lillywhite for a change, successfully completed a 'pair' in the second. Shaw continues:

> It was my turn to follow him in the batting order. When he reached the dressing-room I was in the act of stooping to adjust my leg-guards. Freeman did not see me, and in his vexation at failing to score for the third time he threw his bat violently against the wall of the dressing-room. The bat, fortunately, passed over my head. George was terribly frightened on seeing me, and said his first thought was that he had killed me.

In fact, Lillywhite himself was the man in next, and he joined Griffith with only six to win. Shaw has a much less prosaic version of events:

> When I joined him he hit out and scored a run. On reaching the wicket he threw the bat in the air, delighted at having scored at last, as he thought. But he reckoned without the umpire. That official was so astonished at Lillywhite throwing up his bat that, on being appealed to, he gave him 'run out'. This ruling in turn amazed Lillywhite, who asked the umpire what he meant. The umpire's reply was an outburst of indignation at having his ruling questioned, and he stalked off the field in high dudgeon, vowing that he would act as umpire for these impudent Englishmen no more.

The facts, such as they are, can only be fitted into the dramatic conclusion of the first Philadelphian match. Naturally enough, in the twilight world of Shaw's imagination, Freeman and Lillywhite decided to call the bet off in favour of a friendly drink.

Several professionals from Boston and New York were drafted in for the second match, including Pearson, the umpiring saviour of the first match. The Philadelphia Club, however, was not as

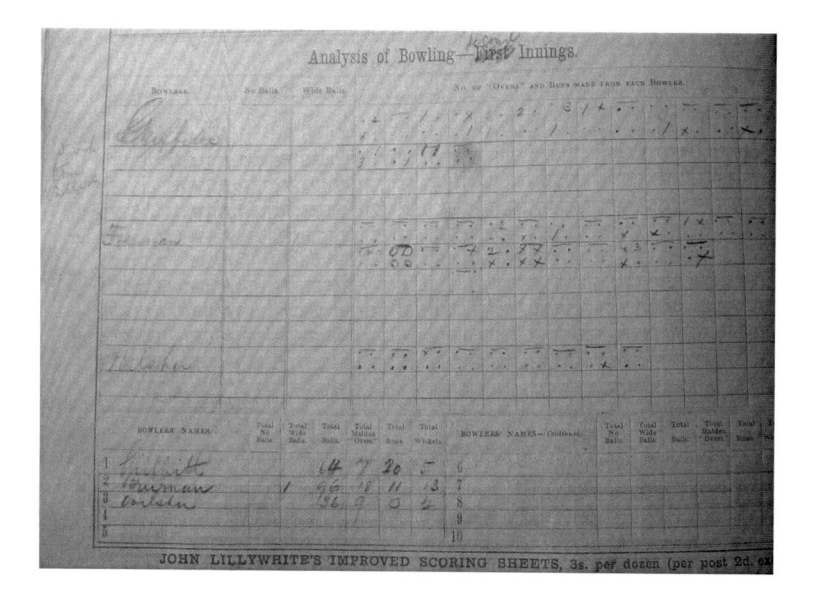

The All-England bowling analysis for the Philadelphia XXII second innings at Nicetown on 6 October 1868. Note Freeman's 13 wickets for 9 runs in 25 four-ball overs, including four wickets in his nineteenth over. Willsher bowled nine consecutive maiden overs and took two wickets.

happy with him as the English squad would have been after he obligingly signalled the crucial 'wide'. Its minutes for 1868 reflect the frustrations felt by committees since the dawn of time with regard to the difficulty in finding the model professional:

> Mr Pearson is undoubtedly a fine cricketer as well as a steady, sober man, and the club has desired much improvement and satisfaction from his services during the past two years. But it must be admitted that he does not come up to the requirements of a first-class professional, either in his bowling, or in the matter of instruction to players.

Certainly, George Newhall did not see fit to use his talents in either innings of the England eleven. Only three bowlers were deployed, which may have been a little short-sighted, as the visitors returned to their best form, especially in a second-wicket stand of 61 in 70 minutes between Jupp and Smith in the first innings after Willsher had won the toss. Despite Charles Newhall's eight for 57, a total of 117 was enough to break the spirit of the Twenty-Two, who managed a total of only 109 in their two innings. Willsher left nothing to chance this time, giving his best performance of the tour so far with fourteen wickets in the match to go with Freeman's eighteen. A margin of defeat of 72 runs was no disgrace, but, with

Dan Newhall's 20 the only double-figure score for the Twenty-Two in the whole match, it was clear that considerable technical work was still needed if Americans were ever to compete with the bat.

Much the same could probably be said of the English professionals with regard to baseball. Monday, 12 October was set aside for a match at Nicetown against the Athletic Club of Philadelphia, and, according to the *Inquirer*, 'a great deal of amusement was afforded the spectators by their queer mistakes in playing the game.' Despite various attempts to even up the odds, the novices were again soundly beaten by 31 to 11, and only the allround play of Smith seems to have come up to scratch.

And so, on to the final leg of the tour and the return match in New York. There, despite meeting the same high-class attack as in the second Philadelphian match, Willsher's men were dominant in an innings victory over a rain-affected four days. Ned and George Freeman ran amok as they demolished 'America' for totals of 70 and 65 in reply to England's 143. Freeman's match haul of 18 wickets meant he had taken an astonishing 106 at an average of just 2.01 on the trip, while his captain, courtesy of a final-match analysis of 17 for 54, totalled 62 wickets at 2.34. The batting figures were less mind-boggling, the doughty John Smith being comfortably the leading scorer with 187 runs at a modest average of 20.77. However, bearing in mind the conditions encountered throughout, one needs to at least double that figure to give an idea of its true value.

All that remained in the week before the *City of Baltimore* left for the return trip was a planned series of baseball matches, and a cricket match between two mixed teams of locals and All-Englanders. In the event, miserably wet weather meant that the only serious occasion was that of 20 October, when nine of the touring party played an 'international' baseball match against the Union Club – not the Atlantics, whose invitation seems never to have been taken up – before 'the largest assemblage ever seen on the St George's cricket grounds since the first appearance of the English cricketers.' Even Willsher got stuck in, impressing by putting out 14 at first base, and overall it was the most improved display of the trip. After two and a half hours of non-stop entertainment, the Union, not without a fight, were victors by 40 to 21. The rain set in for the rest of the trip, curtailing any further sport. After almost nine weeks, the tourists finally arrived back at Liverpool on 3 November, after a 'splendid run of ten days.'

So what did it all mean for the future of American cricket?

Regrettably, it seems not to have been able to halt the decline of the sport in New York. In *Wickets in the West*, Robert Fitzgerald's account of the 1872 tour, he summed up the situation neatly by saying that 'cricket is not a popular game in New York. It has a struggle for existence, and is indebted for life to a few determined Englishmen.' In Philadelphia, on the other hand, interest was considerably stimulated by Willsher's visit, and it could be considered both a sporting and financial success. Indeed, each of the three major clubs made a net profit from the two matches of $850. It was also Pennsylvania's first sight of 'high' bowling, and there is no doubt that Edgar's methods had a real influence on the development of the game in the region, culminating in the heyday of Bart King at the turn of the century. King has himself been credited with the development of swing bowling, using the idea of swerve so beloved of baseball pitchers. Thus the tour contributed not only to the transatlantic exchange of ideas, but also ultimately to the transfer of skills between sports. Baseball may eventually have taken hold even in Philadelphia, but Willsher's legacy remains to this day.

Baseball under way at the Union Baseball Ground in Brooklyn, New York in 1865. Willsher's men watched a match from the pagoda on the left at the start of their tour and played baseball here at its end.

Chapter Twelve
Winding Down

The continued respect in which Willsher was held by all, including the game's establishment, was amply illustrated on his return to England in the winter of 1868/69. In a minute dated 1 December, the managing committee of Kent County Cricket Club resolved that no other professional should be asked to play in all the club's matches, a considerable accolade when we bear in mind that no fewer than six players had been so honoured only four years previously. As it turned out, he had another six full seasons of county cricket left in him, with a couple of farewell appearances in 1875.

Having secured himself gainful employment for a further season, he spent much of the rest of the winter trying to improve the lot of his fellow professionals, in his role as a committee member of the Cricketers' Fund Friendly Society (CFFS). After two seasons without a match played for the benefit of the fund, it was in severe danger of having to be wound up, unless well-attended fixtures were arranged for the coming seasons. Reluctantly, partly at Willsher's instigation, Parr and the other dissenting northerners attended a meeting held in London on New Year's Eve, 1868 to discuss the society's future. It soon became clear that the north-south divide was still very much a live issue in the minds of the older members, who abstained when a resolution was passed to raise weekly sickness payments to £2 per week. Their wish for the dissolution of the Society became clear when Parr, Hayward and Carpenter all refused to have anything to do with proposed North v South matches, a decision which caused the *Sporting Gazette* to vent its spleen in no uncertain terms:

> We dare say it is heretical to make the assertion, but we venture nevertheless to affirm that it would not be difficult to find three as "good men and true" as this pig-headed *trio*. Why don't the youngsters of the North ... throw down the gage to the South? There was cricket – and very superior cricket too – before Parr, Carpenter and Hayward honoured the world by coming into it; and we fancy there will be cricket after they have retired from the scene of their triumphs.

84

Willsher showed his own frustration in a letter to *Bell's Life* on 11 January 1869, albeit written with his perennial optimism:
> Why not grasp the "hand of friendship, and become, as all cricketers ought to be, brothers. It would equally benefit both North and South, and by not doing so we are injuring ourselves only ... . Would Daft kindly undertake to get a North Eleven together to meet the South in a match for the benefit of the fund? I believe most of the leading players in the North would play if asked; it would then show that all of us are doing our best to benefit the society and its members.

Upon reading the letter, the *Sporting Gazette* was almost apoplectic, referring to the 'charming "gush"' of Willsher's 'hand of friendship' offer, which could:
> ... only be attributed to the cheery influence of Christmas festivities. Now, we ask Willsher - and he is a shrewd man, as well as an accomplished master of his art - we ask him, in sober seriousness too, whether in the course of his extensive experience he ever discovered genuine friendship or brotherly feeling amongst professional cricketers? If Willsher cannot answer the question, Daft, the best cricketer and most gentlemanly of the northern school, may.

Happily for the less cynical minded amongst us, brotherly feeling was eventually restored, but not by Daft. It was George Freeman, Edgar's old colleague from their North American trip, who helped him arrange the 1870 fixture already described. Once again, the *éminence grise* had shown statesmanlike qualities at a time of crisis, and in doing so had won vastly more friends than enemies.

Edgar's form never scaled the dizzy heights of 1868 again, but he did enough in the new season, with 64 first-class wickets at 16.06, to merit selection for another overseas tour the next winter. (Modern compilations, though, put him outside the leading twenty in the bowling averages in this particular season.) *The Penny Illustrated Paper* of 11 September 1869 reported the inclusion of the 'Kent veteran' in a putative team bound for the Antipodes on 20 September. Along with six members of the previous year's North American squad, the prized name

Willsher in later years, still with a 'faraway look'.

of W.G.Grace had been secured as a guaranteed crowd-puller, but in the end the trip was aborted and Australian audiences would have to wait another four years for their first sight of cricket's leviathan. A similar line-up was suggested by the *Sporting Gazette* of 12 April 1870, this time as the 'English Eleven who are to visit America in the autumn'. Again, the main drawcard was to be Grace, supplemented by eleven professionals, including Willsher and five of his former team-mates, but again, the tour never took place and it was two more years before Gloucestershire's favourite son accompanied a team of amateurs on a jaunt across the Atlantic. For Willsher, his days in the limelight were slowly drawing to a close, and despite the ego boost provided by these invitations, it was time to think of a future beyond the cricketing stage.

After two decades playing for his beloved Kent, it was only right that something should be done to mark the occasion. Sure enough, 'a select circle of friends' gathered on the evening of 22 December 1869 for the presentation of a 'handsome' gold watch and chain at the Queen's Head, run by Robert Willsher's son William, in Borough, the area just south of London Bridge. 'Long may he live to wear it', said *Bell's Life*. Although this was a fine gesture, surely the 'Lion of Kent' was worth more than this after twenty years of unstinting service? Fortunately, the Kent committee agreed, the minutes of 27 January 1871 recording that it had allowed him 'to announce his benefit at Lord's as being under the patronage of Kent CCC.' This meant that, if for instance the weather intervened in his benefit match, the county would be inclined to help out by arranging a replacement fixture at a local venue. This was crucial in the days when the proceeds from one match, rather than a year-long series of events, formed the bulk of the beneficiary's takings.

Edgar was to have every reason to be grateful for his county's backing, for the weather was indeed unkind when 'The Married' turned out at Lord's against 'The Single' on 10 July 1871. The rain only allowed two, frequently interrupted, days of play, and on the second day the outfield was under water at times. Although the spectators were treated to a classic 189 not out by W.G., carrying his bat, there was simply not enough cricket to create a substantial testimonial fund. Even if the weather had relented, the *Sporting Gazette*, forthright as ever, thought the enterprise was doomed from the start:

> It is our opinion that Willsher's benefit match was a mistake. It is simply incomprehensible that any man of experience in cricket should have supposed that a match between the Married and Single of England (let us be grandiose or

expire) would 'draw'. Who cares whether Mr W.G.Grace is married or not – whether R.Daft is a Benedict or a bachelor ... Willsher's troops of personal friends were almost certain to show; it was the public outside these he was anxious to attract ... .

The fixture was not held again until 1892.

The authorities learnt their lesson, for when they decided to offer 'their bowler' another bite of the cherry, they awarded him a prime fixture in September at Mote Park, his home ground, playing for Kent against an eleven selected by W.G. himself. It had originally been arranged as Kent v Gloucestershire, but the visitors had been unable to raise a full side, and three Kent players filled in. Grace's presence alone, at the end of a phenomenal season in which in first-class cricket he scored ten centuries and 2,739 runs, would guarantee a crowd, but it was their local hero that they would come to support, in their thousands. Grace was already a sporting god at the age of 23, but Willsher had shown his admirers what ordinary mortals could achieve through sheer hard graft. Now all it needed was the weather gods to smile on him.

As it transpired, said *Wisden*, 'The weather during the first two days at Mote Park was splendid, that very charming spot being seen ... to the utmost possible advantage.' The play was equally splendid, although the match was characterised by lax timekeeping according to *The Field* magazine; perhaps there was an end of term feel about things. Grace, as usual, dominated proceedings; indeed, he was on the field throughout the match. After six wickets in Kent's first innings 157, he carried his bat for 81, ensuring that his team's deficit was only 16. The second day belonged to a brilliant century by William Yardley, the scorer of a memorable century in the previous year's Varsity match. When Kent were all out at the close of play, their lead of 255 set up the prospect of an intriguing last day chase for W.G. and his men, and as the local mills closed early on a Saturday, a particularly large attendance was anticipated. Unfortunately for Willsher, rain set in in the early afternoon, and no result was possible, a particular shame as Grace and brother Fred were together at lunch and batting ominously well. All was not lost, though, for 'Willsher stated that the balance in his favour "would be well over £500".' In fact, when *Bell's Life* announced the grand total on 2 March, 1872, it had swollen to £794, the equivalent of about £55,000 today. Curiously, the Lord's match had actually netted more money than the replacement game, and the MCC was the largest single donor. The newspaper hoped that the generosity of the authorities and the public would 'enable the *beneficiaire* to embark in some lucrative business.'

Edgar could be well satisfied with an amount that compared very favourably with the benefits of contemporaries like Tom Emmett (£616) and Edward Pooley (£400), but he would have to make wise investment decisions when he retired to ensure that he did not end up in the workhouse like the former Surrey keeper. In practice, the most likely options open to him were being a publican or a sports goods outfitter, while keeping up a connection with the professional game in some way. This usually entailed umpiring or coaching, and both were something Willsher had already had ample experience of during his long career. In addition to his stint with Lord Enville, he was engaged as a professional by Manchester's Broughton club in 1859, and there are numerous instances of him coaching at public schools and both of the major universities. In May 1862, *Bell's Life* records him playing in a practice match against Rugby School, along with others, such as Cambridgeshire's 'Ducky' Diver, who would have supplemented their income for a few precious weeks by bringing on the next generation of gentleman cricketers. He also merits a brief, but hardly flattering, mention in William Patterson's *Sixty Years of Uppingham Cricket*:

> ... the 'coach' who came in 1868, and again in 1870, was well known in the cricketing world ... no doubt Willsher did his duty, but his ministrations being short, and confined to a period of three weeks of cold weather, and on the soft wickets to be expected so early in the season, little permanent impression was left on the cricket of the school ... Willsher's fee was £5 per week with travelling expenses.

Finally, a tantalising and poignant glimpse of this hand-to-mouth existence comes in the form of two entries in the census of April 1871. The first records Sarah Willsher living with sons Ernest and Edgar junior, and daughters Edith and Alice, at 115 Upper Fant, Maidstone, probably the last family home before a move to Lewisham. The second shows Edgar boarding at 46 High Street, Marlborough, and the most logical conclusion is that he was coaching at the local school, although no records survive from that time.

The harsh reality for Willsher and millions like him was that he would literally have to continue working until he dropped, trying every means possible to keep himself and his family afloat. Although his summer income may just have been enough to sustain them through the winter, he would not have been in a position to refuse local employment when it arose. After his sojourn at his cousin's pub in Borough, this may well have included working for his brother William, who, in *Melville's Maidstone Directory* of 1858, is described as a wine and spirit merchant and landlord of the George Inn on Gabriel's Hill. Whether he continued working in the trade after his brother's death in 1861 is not recorded, but once his benefit had been realised in 1871 he could surely afford one winter off, especially as he was just about to embark on the last big challenge of his career. On 16 December 1871, the *Sporting Gazette* announced that 'Willsher would be available for only two of his county matches and their returns, as he had been engaged as manager and principal bowler for the Prince's ground, Brompton.'[19]

The entrepreneurial brothers George and James Prince had established a social club just north of Milner Street in Chelsea in about 1850, erecting rackets and real tennis courts in 1853. Always with an eye for the main chance, in 1869 the brothers took the lease of an adjoining 13 acre site from the Cadogan Estate to create a cricket ground, croquet lawn and skating rink. With over 700 members from the upper echelons of society, this was a fashionable resort for the London élite, and Edgar would have been comparatively well paid. It was no sinecure, though. Alfred Lubbock, writing in his *Memories of Eton and Etonians*, made it clear what Willsher was up against:

> The two Princes themselves knew absolutely nothing about the game of cricket. Many were the amusing remarks they made on the subject, and although I did my best to persuade them that if they wanted good attendance and gate money, they must produce good cricket, they didn't see it, and thought a band and 'soldier's cricket' was the acme of perfection in this line, and would command a big assembly. As it was, at most of the matches a whole bevy of duchesses and dowagers came down nominally to see the cricket; but, as a rule, they sat with their backs to the game, watching their daughters skating on the asphalte, in happy ignorance all the time that a good hit might at any time catch them full in the small of the back.

Despite the Princes' best efforts, first-class cricket was indeed played on the ground for the first time in May 1872, when the North took on the South. Edgar played for the South, but he had no time to contribute, as the game was washed out after the first

---

[19] Willsher was one of several professional ground bowlers engaged by the Princes between 1872 and 1878, and was identified in *Wisden* as their 'captain'.

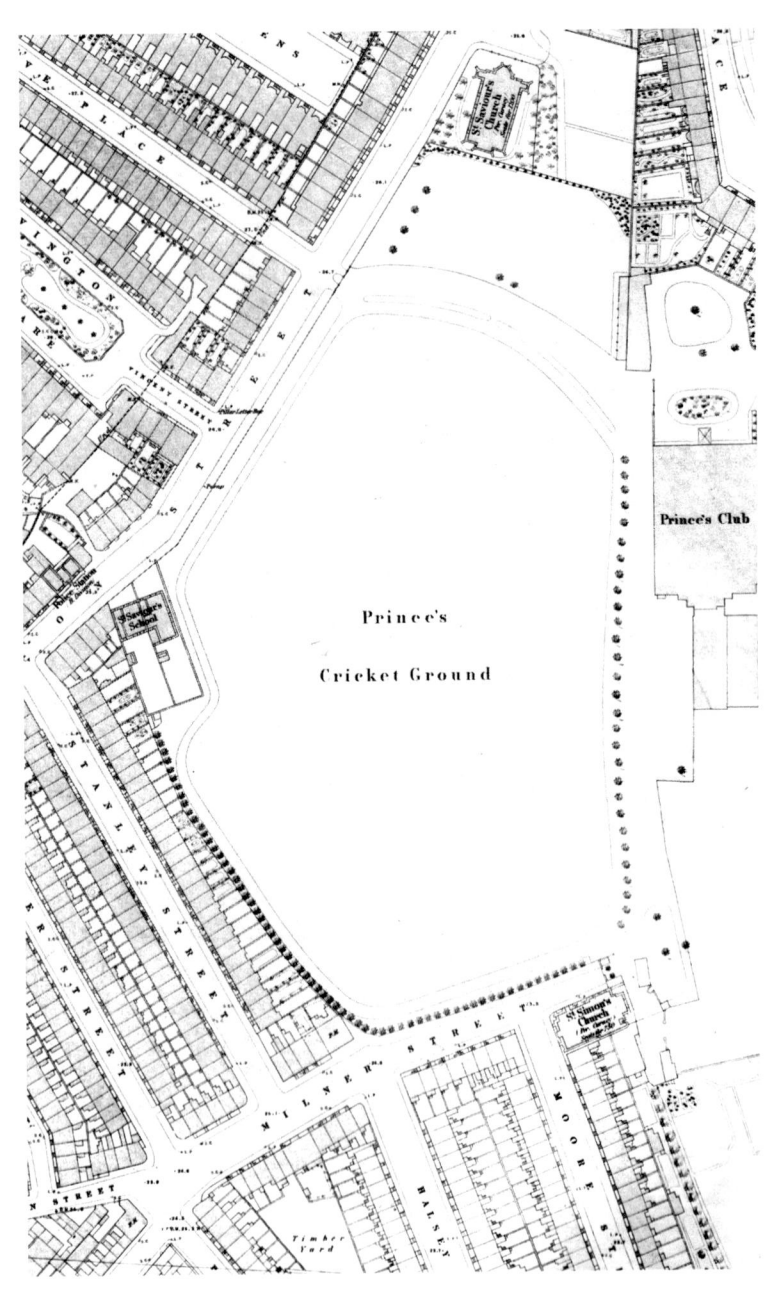

Prince's Cricket Ground in Chelsea during Willsher's time.
He was 'captain' of the ground's professional bowling staff from 1872 to 1878,
playing in two, and umpiring in 21 first-class fixtures here.
With Tom Box, he oversaw its re-turfing in 1874.

day. *Baily's* magazine concurred with Lubbock in its post-match verdict:

> ... while it is likely to be an unrivalled ground for the players, it is anything but agreeable to the spectators. The light, especially in the afternoon, is bad; the wickets are so far off that it is impossible to observe the minutiae of the game and there is not adequate accommodation for such crowds as visit Lord's for the Oxford and Cambridge and Eton and Harrow matches.

Nevertheless, Middlesex decided to adopt Prince's as its home ground, an arrangement that lasted four years until the lack of practice facilities and poor spectator accommodation led to a relocation to Lord's that has lasted to the present day. The Princes had lost a major client due to their joint myopia, and there were to be only five more first-class matches played there after the county left.

In the winter of 1874, the ground was re-turfed under the supervision of Willsher and Thomas Box, the old Sussex wicketkeeper who was now head groundsman. The *Sporting Gazette* of 25 March 1874 reported that the Eton boys wanted to play football on the new ground in the midst of a bout of ice and snow. Eventually, 'they had the good sense to recognise the wisdom of Mr Prince's action, under the advice of Willsher'. Although no harm was done, it was typical of the type of problems Edgar was facing on a daily basis, and it could not have helped Box's chronic heart condition. Sadly, while changing the scoreboard during Middlesex's last match on the ground, against Nottinghamshire in 1876, he collapsed with a heart attack and died three hours later, the match being abandoned as a mark of respect. Unfortunately for Willsher, it was all too symbolic of what was happening to Prince's as a whole, and, after he had umpired the final first-class match on the ground – the Players against the Australians in September 1878, at the end of a wet summer – developers gradually ate away at the site, completely covering it by the end of 1883. By the beginning of 1879, with his professional playing days four years behind him, it was clear that it was time for the veteran to make his own foray into the world of business.

Chapter Thirteen
Epitaph

The first indication that the Willsher family had moved away from Maidstone came in *James Lillywhite's Cricketer's Annual* of 1874, where their address is listed as 110 Amersham Vale, New Cross. Edgar's mother had died in 1871 at the ripe old age of 85, and, with his contract at Prince's starting in the following summer, it made sense to make a permanent move nearer to central London, especially as cousin William was only just down the road in Borough. Non-property owners moved around frequently in Victorian times to get the best rental deals, and the Willshers were no exception. We have several addresses for them in Maidstone, with most of the original buildings still standing, but of the five known in the Lewisham area, none appears to have survived. According to the *South Eastern Gazette*, it was at 10 Commercial Place, Lewisham Road, Greenwich, that Edgar set up a 'cricket outfitting depot' in 1875.

Willsher, like many retired sportsmen through the ages, hoped to trade off his name for at least a few years, until the business had become firmly established. That his name was indeed worth something is shown by an advertisement in *Kelly's Directory* of 1876, placed by Jefferies and Co of Woolwich, tennis-racket and cricket-bat makers. Amongst a list of glowing testimonials is this from Willsher himself, sent from Prince's ground on 28 February 1874:

> The cricketing articles supplied by you to Prince's Club last season gave general satisfaction – the cane-handle bats driving well, the wood being good, and the balls lasting well and keeping their shape.

The fact that this endorsement was still being used in 1882 may simply mean that Jefferies did not spend much time updating their advertising, but it is perfectly conceivable that they gave Willsher favourable rates for its bats, especially as his premises were no more than four miles away. Whatever deals he may have been able to arrange, they were of no lasting benefit, for in 1881, according to Haygarth, 'owing to lack of support, he had to resign his business.'

The reasons for the failure of the business are perhaps not too difficult to find. The United Kingdom's economy was in recession from 1875 to 1880, and Gross Domestic Product did not return to 1874 levels until 1881. The location of the business, away from the people who had known him for a quarter of a century, surely told against him, even though Greenwich is part of Metropolitan Kent. Back in Maidstone, his celebrity would probably have ensured a certain degree of success, but on the outskirts of the big city he was simply another player in an already saturated market.

The simple truth was that he was too late. Others, like his nemesis John Lillywhite, had got there before him. Lillywhite's *Companion* carried full-page advertisements for his 'cricket warehouse' in Euston Square, the forerunner of *Lillywhite's* department store in Piccadilly. Willsher seems never to have been able to afford to advertise. A final reason, in Haygarth's opinion, was lack of support from his former employers. There may be a certain amount of justification for his comments, but Kent was not entirely unsympathetic to Edgar's plight. A committee minute of 12 March 1881 reported that he was 'in a distressed condition' and granted him £20 from the Alfred Mynn Memorial Fund, a trust to which he had himself donated ten shillings when it was founded in 1863. While not being enough to save his business, it was probably all that could be spared from the fund at one time. However, when in February 1882 Willsher applied for a second benefit, the committee judged it 'not expedient' and awarded him just £5, not enough to keep a family of six for more than a few weeks.[20] More locally, a benefit match was organised at Blackheath on 24 September 1881 between a local eleven and eighteen West Kent Wanderers, but there is no record of what the proceeds amounted to.

Edgar was not completely without other sources of income. He umpired regularly in first-class cricket: he had been standing in inter-county matches about four or five times each season from 1864 onwards, and had regularly officiated at Prince's and in games in the Canterbury week, appointed by the Kent club. His services were also secured for four matches of the Australians' tour of 1880. At the end of the 1882 season, in response to dissatisfaction about the standard of umpiring in county cricket, the MCC invited the counties to nominate umpires to form a panel to officiate in county matches. Umpires were not permitted to stand in matches involving clubs with which they were associated and this brought

---

20   No evidence of bankruptcy, as such, has been found.

an end to the previous system wherein each side supplied its own umpire, a potential source of bias. Kent nominated Edgar and he was duly appointed to the first-ever county umpires list along with fifteen others for the 1883 season. A total of 62 county matches were played that year but he stood in only two, both at Hove towards the season's end, so it was hardly a remunerative activity. He remained on the list for two more seasons, officiating in six county games in 1884 and nine in 1885. He evidently stood in minor matches too, perhaps helped by *Wisden* listing him in its section 'Umpires and where to find them'.

He also continued to play for a diverse mix of teams in non first-class cricket, and he may have received some form of recompense for these appearances. Among the latter was a match, recorded in the *Essex Standard* of 31 July 1880, in which Willsher captained an 'Eleven of England' against twenty-two of Chelmsford. He proved that he still retained some of his old powers by taking nine wickets in Chelmsford's first innings, but the paper reported that the match 'did not prove a success financially', presumably because the 'England' eleven was anything but representative. His final match as a player appears to have been for 'Twenty Colts of the County and a Captain' against an eleven of Kent, as reported by the *Northern Echo* on 11 May 1885. Whether or not he was the captain mentioned, we are not told, but we do know that Willsher, batting at No.19, scored a duck, and took one wicket, that of George Hearne, as Kent completed an easy victory. Fittingly, Hearne was also a left-arm bowler, and was to go on to take 570 wickets for his county. This was not quite Edgar's last appearance on a cricket field, as from 10 to 12 August he was at Derby umpiring, with the Lancastrian 'Kerr' Coward, an undistinguished draw between the home county and Yorkshire. Less than two months later, he was dead.

Edgar Willsher passed away at his final residence of 18 Lethbridge Road, Lewisham, on 7 October 1885, surrounded by his family. He was not quite 57. His death certificate says that he died of 'exhaustion and carcinoma hepatis', or liver cancer in today's terminology. As the *South Eastern Gazette* recorded, his demise had appeared inevitable for several months:

> ... it had been evident that his health was failing and though he had been able to officiate as umpire in the earlier fixtures of the year, he was compelled to refuse several later engagements, and since August had been confined to his bed without the slightest hope of recovery.

The fickle nature of fame is indicated by complete lack of coverage in the local Lewisham press, and only cursory mentions in the national newspapers. *Bell's Life* produced a more lengthy obituary, concluding that 'few if any professionals were more esteemed by cricketers of all grades than was poor Willsher', and *Cricket* paid substantial tribute in its edition of 29 October, acknowledging that 'the bowler ... who surpasses or equals Ted Willsher will indeed be a "demon".'

If journalists had short memories, there was no such problem with his fellow cricketers, who turned out *en masse* to pay their respects at his funeral service, held at Ladywell Cemetery in Lewisham on 12 October. Arthur Haygarth has left us a detailed description, telling of how a group of mourners, including the brothers Alec and George Hearne of Kent,

> ... formed two lines, and followed the coffin into the chapel ... on reaching the graveside everyone felt gratified to observe that Lord Harris had not permitted political engagements to absorb his whole attention, but had found time to pay a tribute of respect to the memory of one who on the cricket field had so long and so well upheld the honour of the county to which they were both attached. The coffin, which was of plain oak ... was covered with floral tributes of loving friends. ... A memorial stone was subsequently placed over the grave ... it having been subscribed for by Lord Harris and one hundred gentlemen and professional cricketers of England. It takes the form of a cross, on the transverse being the words, 'Thy will be done'.

When the author visited the cemetery in the summer of 2009, the memorial, impossible to find without a detailed map, was buried deep within a patch of luxuriant grassland. It has long since lost its cross, but, after a bit of judicious grass-flattening, it yields its secrets to the all-seeing eye of the digital camera. One can still faintly make out the original carved inscription on the base, which reads:

> SACRED TO THE MEMORY OF EDGAR WILLSHER CRICKETER WHO PLAYED WITH HIS NATIVE COUNTY KENT FOR OVER A QUARTER OF A CENTURY DIED 7TH OCTOBER 1885 THIS STONE WAS ERECTED TO HIS MEMORY BY A GREAT NUMBER OF THOSE WHO HAD WITNESSED HIS BRILLIANT PERFORMANCES IN THE CRICKET FIELD AND WHO RESPECTED THE STERLING QUALITIES OF HIS CHARACTER

Last throw of the dice. Willsher ran the billiard room at this pub, the George and Dragon at Blackheath, at the end of his life. Photograph taken in 2009.

Willsher's grave in Ladywell Cemetery, Lewisham. The text (see page 95) gives details of its inscription.

Whilst it must have been gratifying for Edgar's widow to know that her husband had been held in such high regard, Sarah's priority was to ensure that she and her four children were provided for. She obtained the grant of probate on 6 November, at which point Edgar's gross estate was valued at £175, about £14,000 at today's values. Although a reasonable sum, it was hardly a fortune. His benefit money and other savings had gradually dwindled through the failure of his shop, and indeed that of his final business venture, a billiard room upstairs at the George and Dragon pub on Blackheath Hill, which he had opened in October 1883. Fortunately, all of the Willsher children seem to have been employed; in the 1881 census, eldest child Ernest is described as a 'turner at marine engine factory', while daughters Edith and Alice are 'dressmaker' and 'milliner' respectively. Only youngest son Edgar junior is without occupation. By 1891, his siblings having flown the nest, Edgar is head of household and a clerk of works, a job that would have enabled him to look after his mother in a respectable fashion. By the time of her death in 1895, Edgar too has moved out, having married at the end of 1891. Regrettably, after his death in 1915, the trail runs cold, and no direct living descendants have so far been traced.

The question remains as to what sort of legacy the Willsher family would now have to look back on from the perspective of the twenty-first century. Undoubtedly, from a purely playing point of view, what stands out is just how good a bowler he was, as attested by all his great contemporaries. If Test cricket had begun just a few years earlier, there can be no shadow of doubt that he would have been an England regular, and consequently his posthumous reputation would have been that much higher. Instead, he is remembered as the man who was no-balled for bowling above the shoulder in a major match in 1862, leading to the modern era of over-arm bowling. As such, he can be seen as a technical pioneer, pushing the limits of what is acceptable in a game steeped in the tradition of 'fair play'. The question of what constitutes illegal bowling still haunts the game today, and so Willsher's actions continue to resonate with a modern audience, even though it is now hard to see what all the fuss was about.

However, perhaps Willsher should ultimately be remembered as someone who, through word and deed, fought for the right of all professional cricketers to be treated fairly and with dignity. Time after time, we see him standing up for his 'brothers', working like a shop steward to present a united front to, and earn the respect of, the establishment. Seen in this light, the events of August

1862 were a part of his campaign for the serious treatment of the professional's voice. We see this continued in his work for the CFFS and the USEE, and the esteem in which he was held by his peers was clearly reflected in his selection for that momentous tour of 1868. What he may have lacked in tactical acumen was more than made up for by his diplomacy skills and ability to get on with people from all walks of life, all of which helped him to play a major part in the ending of the north-south schism. So great was his influence throughout the country that, in a letter to *Bell's Life* promoting the James Southerton Memorial Fund in July 1880, he felt able to write:

> I think I may promise for the whole of the South of England professional cricketers, and I should not much mind promising for the North of England cricketers too, though I have not had time to consult them, that we all will do our best.

It was a testament to Willsher's generosity of spirit that he should be involved in the effort to provide for a fellow player's family at a time when his own business was struggling, and when he was no longer playing at the highest level himself. Above all, it reflected his commitment to fairness both on and off the field; equality between batsman and bowler, and quality of life for professionals whether young or old, able-bodied or sick. At a time when the continued existence of 'the spirit of cricket' is frequently called into question, it is salutary to be reminded of what that spirit actually is. In conclusion, there is no better summary of Willsher the man than this quote from an article written by Victorian moraliser Frederick Gale for the *Boy's Own Paper* of 3 September 1881, concerning the close finish of the Gentlemen v Players match of 1869:

> The game now mentioned was stopped for a minute whilst Edgar Willsher, the captain, took Pooley out a glass of water for the purpose, backbiters thought, of 'fiddling for time'. But I, the writer, can tell you how the backbiters wronged him, for the glass of water was an excuse for giving Pooley his 'riding orders', which were worthy of a real cricketer like Edgar Willsher, and they were as follows: 'Win the match if you can, but don't play for a draw.'

Acknowledgements

Inevitably with a project of this kind, there are numerous people to thank, and a totally comprehensive list would be beyond the author's limited memory capacity. However, he has tried to include everyone whose contribution was significant enough to stick in the aforesaid neuron-derived database. Apologies in advance for any unintended omissions.

Starting with the American side of operations, special mention must be made of my gracious hosts, the Costa-Baker family. Things would have been a lot more complicated without them. The staff of the New York Public Library and the Historical Society of Pennsylvania were extremely helpful, and I am eternally grateful for the unceasing efforts and enthusiasm of Joe Lynn and Kathleen Burns at the C.C.Morris Library. Pat Kelly at the National Baseball Museum helped with picture research, and Andrew Hignell and Roger Gibbons made the trip possible by expediting my ACS research grant.

Back in the United Kingdom, staff at Cambridge University Library, the British Library at Colindale, the Surrey History Centre, the Kensington and Chelsea Local Studies Centre and the Kent County Archives, as well as David Robertson at Kent CCC and Sandy Haynes at Enville Hall, all pointed me in the right direction. Derek Carlaw also provided me with some crucial information from the Kent CCC archives, while Jack Gillett was kind enough to send a family tree amongst other material. Ian Lambert helped tremendously with local newspaper research.

As far as the actual writing process is concerned, Willie Sugg and Roger Heavens gave much sound advice as the manuscript developed, and contributed materially to drafts in the final stages. David Jeater was a perceptive and persistent editor; and David Kelly and Willie Sugg have undertaken the proofreading. Derek Underwood was kind enough to take time from his busy schedule to provide a foreword. Roger Mann has contributed several illustrations. Last but not least a big thank you to all family and friends who expressed an interest, including my trusty travelling companion and stenographer-in-chief, Janine-Jacquline St.Léger.

G.P.
Ely, Cambridgeshire

Bibliography

Principal sources consulted are as follows:

1 Newspapers and journals
Baily's Magazine; *Bell's Life in London*; *Boston Evening Transcript* (U.S.A.); *Boston Herald* (U.S.A.); *Boy's Own Magazine*; *Brooklyn Daily Eagle* (U.S.A.); *Cricket: A Weekly Record*; *Daily News*; *The Era*; *Essex Standard*; *Every Boy's Magazine*; *The Field*; *Harper's Weekly* (U.S.A.); *Maidstone Journal*; *Montreal Gazette* (Canada); *New York Clipper*, *New York Commercial Advertiser*, *New York Herald*, *New York Times*, *North America and US Gazette* (all U.S.A.); *Northern Echo*; *Penny Illustrated Paper*, *Philadelphia Inquirer* (U.S.A.): *Sheffield Independent*; *South Eastern Gazette*; *Spirit of the Times* (U.S.A.); *Sporting Gazette*; *Sporting Life*; *The Times*.

2 Annuals
Frederick Lillywhite's Guide to Cricketers
James Lillywhite's Cricketers' Annual
John Lillywhite's Cricketers' Companion
Wisden Cricketers' Almanack

3 Books
Adelman, Melvin, *A Sporting Time: New York City and the Rise of Modern Athletics 1820-70*, University of Illinois Press, 1986
Bettesworth, W.A., *Chats on the Cricket Field*, Merritt and Hatcher, 1910
Bettesworth, W.A., *The Walkers of Southgate*, Methuen, 1900
Brodribb, Gerald, *Felix on the Bat*, Eyre and Spottiswoode, 1962
Caffyn, William, *Seventy-one Not Out*, Blackwood and Sons, 1899
Cashman, Richard, *The 'Demon' Spofforth*, NSW University Press, 1990
Cobbett, William, *Rural Rides*, William Cobbett, 1830
Daft, Richard, *Kings of Cricket*, Simpkin, Marshall, 1893
Down, Michael, and West, Derek, *Sketches at Lord's*, Collins, 1990
Fitzgerald, Robert, *Wickets in the West*, Tinsley, 1873
Frindall, Bill, *The Wisden Book of Cricket Records* (Fourth Edition), Headline, 1998
Glover, Judith, *Place Names of Kent*, Batsford, 1976
Grace, W.G., *Cricket*, J.W.Arrowsmith, 1891
Harris, Lord, *A Few Short Runs*, John Murray, 1921
Harris, Lord, *The History of Kent County Cricket*, Eyre and Spottiswoode, 1907
Haygarth, Arthur, *Frederick Lillywhite's Scores and Biographies Volumes 1-15*, various publishers, various years
Kirsch, George B., *The Creation of American Team Sports*, University of Illinois, 1989

Lester, John A., *A Century of Philadelphian Cricket*, University of Pennsylvania Press, 1951
Lillywhite, Fred, *The English Cricketers' Trip to Canada and the United States*, F.Lillywhite, 1860
Lubbock, Alfred, *Memories of Eton and Etonians*, John Murray, 1899
Mangan, J.A., *Pleasure, Profit, Proselytism: British Culture and Sport at Home and Abroad: 1700-1914*, Routledge, 1988
Martin, Edward Winslow, *The Secrets of the Great City*, Jones Bros, 1868
Melville, Tom, *The Tented Field*, Bowling Green, 2000
Milton, Howard, *Cricket Grounds of Kent*, ACS Publications, 1992
Morrah, Patrick, *Alfred Mynn and the Cricketers of His Time*, Eyre and Spottiswoode, 1968
Newhall, George, *The Cricket Grounds of Germantown and a Plea for the Game*, 1910
Official Reports on the International Cricket Fetes at Philadelphia in 1868 and 1872, J. B.Lippincott, 1873
Patterson, W.S, *Sixty Years of Uppingham Cricket*, Longmans, Green, 1909
Peverelly, Charles A., *Book of American Pastimes* (Second Edition), Peverelly, 1866
Pullin, A.W., *Alfred Shaw, Cricketer: His Career and Reminiscences*, Cassell and Co, 1902
Pullin, A.W., *Talks With Old English Cricketers*, William Blackwood, 1900
Pycroft, James, *Cricketana*, Longman, 1865
Rae, Simon, *W. G. Grace*, Faber and Faber, 1998
Rait Kerr, R.S., *The Laws of Cricket*, Longmans Green, 1950
Reaney, P.H. and Wilson, R.M., *A Dictionary of English Surnames* (Revised Edition), Oxford University Press, 1997
Sentance, P.David., *Cricket in America, 1710-2000*, McFarland and Co., 2006
Sissons, Ric, *The Players*, Kingswood, 1988
West, Derek, *The Elevens of England*, Darf, 1988

4 Websites

www.kentarcheaology.co.uk
www.ancestry.co.uk
www.cricketarchive.com
http://hansard.millbank.systems.com
www.nationalarchives.gov.uk/currency
www.polofarm.org/cricket/historyintro.html

Appendix
Career Statistics

The statistical details given below relate to Edgar Willsher's performances in matches identified as first-class by the Association of Cricket Statisticians and Historians and listed in its 1996 publication Complete First-Class Match List: Volume I, 1801-1914.

First-Class Cricket: Batting and Fielding

Season	M	I	NO	Runs	HS	Ave	100	50	Ct
1850	1	2	1	8	8	8.00	-	-	1
1851	2	3	1	30	24	15.00	-	-	1
1852	5	10	0	104	30	10.40	-	-	1
1853	6	12	0	86	25	7.16	-	-	5
1854	8	15	1	177	41	12.64	-	-	10
1855	7	14	0	136	24	9.71	-	-	7
1856	8	14	1	137	37	10.53	-	-	5
1857	10	19	2	167	47	9.82	-	-	13
1858	6	11	1	113	33	11.30	-	-	5
1859	14	23	2	172	21	8.19	-	-	11
1860	14	22	2	381	73	19.05	-	4	21
1861	15	27	5	437	59	19.86	-	1	11
1862	13	24	1	319	54	13.86	-	1	17
1863	17	31	3	494	89	17.64	-	3	8
1864	16	30	3	288	37*	10.66	-	-	17
1865	14	26	5	342	58	16.28	-	1	10
1866	11	16	3	170	34	13.07	-	-	18
1867	13	21	4	267	46	15.70	-	-	15
1868	16	28	5	246	33*	10.69	-	-	21
1869	15	22	6	293	70	18.31	-	2	6
1870	17	31	4	226	36	8.37	-	-	6
1871	13	24	2	157	34	7.13	-	-	6
1872	9	16	3	130	45*	10.00	-	-	3
1873	8	16	4	88	21*	7.33	-	-	7
1874	7	13	4	115	34	12.77	-	-	6
1875	2	3	0	6	5	2.00	-	-	2
Totals	**267**	**473**	**63**	**5089**	**89**	**12.41**	**-**	**12**	**233**

Notes: Willsher played all his first-class cricket in England. He was dismissed 195 times bowled (48%); 172 times caught (41%); 23 times stumped (6%); 18 times run out (4%) and twice hit wicket. He was never out lbw. He was dismissed most often by James Southerton (24 times), James Grundy (19), John Wisden (18), and George Tarrant (17). He played 147 matches for Kent, scoring 3,221 runs at 13.14 and taking 124 catches.

First-Class Cricket: Bowling

Season	O	M	R	W	BB	Ave	5i	10m
1850				4	4-?	?	-	-
1851	80	15	70	11	6-?	17.70	1	-
1852	78.3	26	155	5	2-22	31.00	-	-
1853	157.2	61	198	21	6-47	14.14	1	-
1854	318.1	136	414	32	7-28	12.93	2	-
1855	284.3	27	392	21	7-22	18.66	1	1
1856	415.2	167	592	66	7-37	10.76	7	4
1857	623.3	293	782	71	6-22	11.01	5	1
1858	211.3	86	323	29	7-53	11.13	3	1
1859	579.3	246	790	79	7-51	10.00	8	2
1860	699	347	681	80	8-16	9.32	5	1
1861	861.2	373	1014	87	8-27	11.65	5	1
1862	681	309	845	79	6-32	10.69	8	1
1863	1035.2	474	1339	80	7-22	16.73	4	-
1864	871.2	386	1065	79	7-47	13.48	6	-
1865	614.2	276	715	47	7-43	16.25	3	2
1866	578.1	272	688	52	7-24	13.23	3	1
1867	605.3	294	755	51	8-104	14.80	2	1
1868	999.3	529	1128	113	7-44	9.98	12	6
1869	816.3	416	1028	64	7-54	16.06	6	2
1870	918.3	508	1062	84	7-22	12.64	9	2
1871	756.1	401	935	70	7-46	13.35	7	2
1872	428.2	210	570	30	5-89	19.00	2	-
1873	379	191	473	34	6-42	13.91	3	1
1874	290.1	139	434	35	7-22	12.40	4	1
1875	30.3	14	45	5	4-32	9.00	-	-
Totals	**13316.3**	**6196**	**16493**	**1329**	**8-16**	**12.78**	**107**	**30**

Notes: Overs were of four balls throughout Willsher's first-class career. He took his wickets at the rate of one per 41.10 balls and conceded runs at a rate equivalent to 1.86 runs per six-ball over. Of his 1,329 wickets, 710 (53%) were bowled; 567 (43%) were caught; 28 (2%) were stumped; 21 (2%) were lbw and three were hit wicket. He dismissed three batsmen twenty-five times or more; these were J.Grundy 44, T.Lockyer 26, and G.Griffith 25. For Kent he took 786 wickets at 12.55, including 64 five-wicket returns.

First-Class Cricket: Fifty runs or more in an innings (12)

Score	For	Opponent	Venue	Season
53	Kent[1]	MCC	Lord's	1860
73	Players[1]	Gentlemen	Lord's	1860
55	All-England XI[1]	United England XI	The Oval	1860
52	Kent[1]	Sussex	Tunbridge Wells	1860
59	Kent[1]	Surrey	The Oval	1861
54	England[1]	Surrey	The Oval	1862
59*	Kent[1]	Surrey	Hove	1863
77	Players[1]	Gentlemen	The Oval	1863
89	Kent[2]	Sussex	Sandgate	1863
58	Kent[1]	Surrey	The Oval	1865
70	Kent[1]	Surrey	Crystal Palace	1869
57*	Players of South[1]	Gentlemen of South	The Oval	1869

Notes: The index figures [1] and [2] in this and the following table indicate the innings in which the feat was achieved. The ground at Hove was the Brunswick Ground, and at Tunbridge Wells the Higher Common Ground.

First-Class Cricket: Six wickets or more in an innings (58)

Analysis	For	Opponent	Venue	Season
37-?-?-6	Kent	England[1]	Canterbury	1851
40-18-47-6	Gentlemen of England	United England XI[1]	Hove	1853
25-6-28-7	Kent	United England XI[1]	Gravesend	1854
26-?-22-7	Kent	Sussex[2]	Hove	1855
25-11-37-7	South	North[2]	Lord's	1856
30-15-33-6	England	MCC[2]	Lord's	1856
?-?-?-6	Kent and Sussex	England[1]	Canterbury	1856
27-27-22-6	Kent and Sussex	England[2]	Lord's	1857
34-12-46-6	Kent and Sussex	England	Canterbury	1857
39-10-66-6	Gentlemen of Kent	Gentlemen of England[1]	Lord's	1858
36-17-53-7	Kent	Sussex[1]	Tunbridge Wells	1858
24-14-18-6	Gentlemen of Kent	Gentlemen of England[1]	Lord's	1859
31-8-64-7	Gentlemen of Kent	Gentlemen of England[2]	Lord's	1859
43.2-17-51-7	Kent	Sussex[1]	Hove	1859
16-10-14-6	Gentlemen of Kent	Gentlemen of England[1]	Canterbury	1859
24-13-29-6	Players	Gentlemen[2]	Lord's	1860
41-31-16-8	Kent	England[1]	Canterbury	1860
58-?-71-6	South	North[2]	Rochdale	1860
57.2-21-89-6	England	Surrey[1]	The Oval	1861
39-15-49-6	Kent	Surrey[2]	Maidstone	1861
33-25-27-8	Kent	England[1]	Canterbury	1861
26.2-9-35-6	South	North[1]	Old Trafford	1862
55.2-24-86-6	South	North[1]	Lord's	1862
34-10-32-6	Kent	Yorkshire[2]	Cranbrook	1862
32-14-49-6	England	Surrey[1]	The Oval	1862
27.1-16-22-7	MCC	Cambridgeshire[2]	Lord's	1863
62-29-63-6	Kent	Nottinghamshire[1]	Trent Bridge	1864
33-15-44-6	Players of South	Gentlemen of South[2]	The Oval	1864
39-11-47-7	Kent	Surrey[1]	The Oval	1864
42.1-18-43-7	Kent	Sussex[1]	Hove	1865
23-16-19-6	Kent	Yorkshire[1]	Sheffield (BL)	1865
15-10-9-6	Kent	Yorkshire[2]	Sheffield (BL)	1865
80-41-72-6	Kent	Sussex[2]	Gravesend	1866
30.2-18-24-7	South of Thames	North of Thames[1]	Canterbury	1866
35.3-19-37-6	South of Thames	North of Thames[2]	Canterbury	1867
50.2-17-104-8	Kent	Gentlemen of MCC[1]	Canterbury	1867
47.3-26-57-7	England	MCC[1]	Lord's	1868
51.2-26-52-6	Kent	Sussex[1]	Hove	1868
38.3-14-69-6	Kent	Sussex[2]	Hove	1868
31.2-23-18-6	Kent	Surrey[1]	Gravesend	1868
22.2-5-44-7	Players of South	Gentlemen of South[1]	The Oval	1868
53-33-46-6	Kent	Gentlemen of MCC[2]	Canterbury	1868
34-15-39-6	Kent	Surrey[2]	The Oval	1868
31-20-22-6	Kent	Sussex[2]	Gravesend	1868
22.1-6-53-6	Kent	Surrey[1]	Crystal Palace	1869
43-21-54-7	Kent	Sussex[1]	Tunbridge Wells	1869
31.2-16-22-7	Kent	Surrey[2]	Maidstone	1870

48-33-32-6	Kent	Gentlemen of MCC[1]	Canterbury	1870
51.1-28-63-6	United South XI	United North XI[1]	The Oval	1870
42-24-50-7	Kent	Sussex[2]	Crystal Palace	1870
66-37-64-7	South	North[1]	Dewsbury	1870
36-16-93-6	South	North[2]	Lord's	1871
27-13-46-7	South	North[2]	Canterbury	1871
66-35-93-6	Kent	Gentlemen of MCC[1]	Canterbury	1871
44.2-23-42-6	Kent	Lancashire[1]	Gravesend	1873
35-18-36-6	Kent	Derbyshire[1]	Wirksworth	1874
16-7-22-7	Kent	Derbyshire[2]	Wirksworth	1874
25.2-6-55-7	Kent	Lancashire[1]	Old Trafford	1874

Notes: Overs were of four balls throughout Willsher's first-class career. In all the instances listed above the ground at Canterbury was the St Lawrence Ground; at Hove it was the Brunswick Ground; at Tunbridge Wells it was the Higher Common Ground.

Umpiring

Edgar Willsher stood in 102 first-class matches, one in 1859, one in 1861, and then between three and five in most seasons from 1864 to 1885. It is possible that he stood in other first-class matches where umpires' names have been lost.

William Willsher

Edgar's older brother William, born at Rolvenden on 12 October 1814, played in one first-class match, for Kent v Surrey at Preston Hall, Aylesford in July 1847. Batting at eleven he was dismissed twice for nought, and did not bowl. He took one catch, the older Tom Sewell off the bowling of W.R.Hillyer, for three. He died at Barming, Kent on 30 November 1861, aged 47.

Sources: www.cricketarchive.com, Wisden Cricketers' Almanack

Index

A page number in bold indicates an illustration.

All-England Eleven 20, 24, 25, 26, 27, 28, 29, 31, **32**, 37, 39, 50, 51, 56, 58
All England XI (in North America) 55, 61, 66, 67, 71, 72, 77, 78, 81, 82
Anderson, George **32**
Ashford, Kent 7, 34
Aylesford CC 12, 13, 14
Australia 51, 53, 56, 86
Australians (touring side) 51, 91, 93

Bailey, T.E. 22
Baily's Magazine 33, 91
Baker, W.de C. 31
Baseball 56, 62, 63, 64, 67, 69, 71, 72, 74, 82, 83
Beagley, Thomas 45
Bearsted, Kent 12, 14, 15,16
Bedser, A.V. 18
Bell's Life journal 16, 24, 28, 33, 36, 37, 39, 40, 43, 45, 46, 48, 51, 53, 60, 85, 86, 87, 88, 95, 98
Benenden, Kent 10-11, 16
Bennett, George 32
Bergenwood, New York 62
Bettesworth, W.A. 40, 55
Bickley, John 29
Blackheath, Kent 93, 97
Bligh, Hon Edward 32
Bligh, Hon Henry 32
Bligh, Hon I.F.W. 32
'Blink Bonny' 37-38
Body Mass Index (BMI) 21
Boston, Massachusetts 58, 71, 75, 80
Boston XXII cricket team 71, 72
Boston, Riverside Park 71, 72
Box, Thomas 25, 91
Boy's Own Magazine/Paper 46, 98
Bridge House Hotel, Southwark 49
British North America Act 1867 69
Broadbridge, James 35
Brooklyn Atlantics Baseball Club 67, **67**, 82
Brooklyn Daily Eagle newspaper 63, 64
Broughton, R.J.P. 47
Brown University, Providence 71
Burbridge, Frederick 39

Cadwalader, C.E. 76
Caesar, Julius 26, **50**
Caffyn, William 18, 19, 21, 22, 25, 26, 36, 53
Cambridge, Massachusetts 71
Cambridgeshire CCC 18, 56, 57, 88
Cambridge University CC 29, 40, 47, 87, 91
Canada 53, 55, 69, 72

Canada cricket team 62, 64
Canterbury, Beverley Ground 12, 31
Canterbury, Kent 12, 15, 16, 25, 31, 32
Canterbury 'week' 31, 93
Captain McGowan (horse) 71
Carpenter, R.P. **32**, 53, 56, 84
Cashman, Richard 18
'Charitable Cricketer, A' 36, 37
Charlwood, H.R.J. **54**, **57**, 58, 77, 78
Chatham, Kent 14
Chelmsford XXII cricket team 94
Chessenden House, Rolvenden 8, **9**
Chilston Park, Kent 14
City of Baltimore, S.S. 59, **59**, 80, 82
Clarke, Alfred **32**, 53, 59
Clarke, William 24, 26, 27, 53
Clay, R.W. 76
Cobbett, William 7
Coward, Cornelius 94
Cranbrook, Kent 16, 28
Cricketers' Fund Friendly Society 28, 29, 85, 98
Cricket magazine 19, 48
Crystal Palace, Sydenham 51

Daft, Richard 19, 36, 56, 84
Daily News newspaper 53
Dark, J.H. 29
Dean, James sen 28, 29
Derby, County Ground 94
Diver, A.J.D. 88
Dudley XXII cricket team 30

East Kent cricket team 16
Emmett, Thomas 21, 88
England 31, 32, 49, 58, 60, 84, 95
England XI cricket team 15, 16, 22, 25, 28, 33, 35, 37, 39, 40, 42, 43, 51, 55, 94
England Test team 57, 97
Enville, Staffordshire 27, 29, **30**, 31, 38
Era, The newspaper 16, 18, 43
Eton College 51, 89, 91
Everett House Hotel, New York 60-61
Every Boy's Magazine 48
Exhibition of 1851, Great 24

Factory Act 1850 24
Fenner, F.P. 28
Felix, Nicholas 15, 24
Fitzgerald, R.A. 47, 83
Flintoff, Andrew 18
Freeman, George 18, 21, 57, **57**, 60, 66, 70, 72, 76, 77, 78, 80, 81, 82, 84

106

Index

Gale, Frederick 98
Gentlemen 26, 28, 32, 43, 98
Gentlemen of England XI 25
Gentlemen of South XI 53
Gentlemen of Surrey XI 50
George IV, King 31
George and Dragon, Blackheath Hill 96, **96**, 97
George Inn, Maidstone 89
Germantown CC, Philadelphia 56, 74, 76
Gloucestershire CCC 86, 87
Grace, E.M. 50
Grace, W.G. 22, 50, 51, 86
Grant, President Ulysses S. 74
Gravesend, Kent 25, 27, 28
Greenwich, Kent 92, 93
Grey, Hon G.H. *see* Stamford, Earl of
Griffith, George 36, **50**, 54, 56, **57**, 60, 70, 72, 77, 78, 79, 80
Grimston, Hon Robert 37, 38
Grundy, James 25, 39
Guy, Joseph 25
Gybbon-Monypenny, Thomas 8

Hair, D.B. 40
Hambledon Club 34
Hampshire CCC 20, 26, 45
Hargrave, Joseph 76
Harper's Weekly magazine 55
Harris, (fourth) Baron 10, 21, 22, 95
Harrow School 91
Harvard University, Cambridge 71
Haygarth, Arthur 10, 12, 13, 92, 93, 95
Hayward, Thomas **32**, 56, 84
Hearne, Alec 95
Hearne, George 94, 95
Hemsted Park, Benenden 10
Hillyer, W.R. 13, 15, 24
Hinkly, Edmund 16, 20
Hoboken, New Jersey 62
Hodges, T.Twisden 11
Hole House, Rolvenden 8
Hollands, Frederick 32, 37
Hove, Sussex 28, 94
Humphrey, Thomas 39, **50**, **54**, 57, **57**, 65, 71, 77

Inman Line (shipping) 59
Ipswich CC 25
Islington, Cattle Market Ground 50
I Zingari 75

Jackson, John 18, 19, 21, **32**, 56
Jefferies and Co (Woolwich) 92
Johnson, M.G. 49
Johnston, John (father-in-law) 31
Jupp, Henry **50**, **54**, 57, **57**, 65, 71, 72, 77, 78, 81

Kent 8, 15, 16, 26, 34, 37, 51, 93, 95
Kent and Surrey XI 42
Kent and Sussex XI 22, 28
Kent Colts XXII 94
Kent County XI 10, 13, 15, 16, 22, 25, 27, 28, 31, 35, 37

Kent CCC 13, 33, 39, 40, 45, 46, 64, 84, 85, 86, 87, 93, 94, 95
Kentish Gazette newspaper 14, 18
King, J.B. 83
Knickerbocker CC, Montreal 63
Knight, W.H. 25, 51

Ladywell Cemetery, Lewisham 95, **96**
Law 10 34, 36, 37, **40**, 42m 43, 45, 46, 47
Lewes, Dripping Pan 50
Lewisham, Kent 88, 92, 94, 95
Lillywhite's Cricketers'Annual, James 92
Lillywhite's Cricketers' Companion, Fredk. 10, 48, 59, 93
Lillywhite's Guide, Fredk. 28, 50
Lillywhite, Frederick 56, 59
Lillywhite, F.William 24, 33, 36
Lillywhite, James jun **50**, **54**, 57, **57**, 59, 60, 65, 72, 77, 78, 79, 80
Lillywhite, John 10, 34, 36, 37, 38, 39-42, **42**, 43, 48, 49, 59, 93
Lincoln, President Abraham 22, 74
'Lion of Kent' 21, 34, 86
Little Halden Farm, Rolvenden 8, **9**, 10
Liverpool, Lancashire 59, 80, 82
Lockyer, Thomas 39, **50**
Lord's Cricket Ground 13, 16, 28, 29, 32, 35, 37, 38, 39, 42, 45, 47, 48, 51, 86, 87, 91
Lubbock, Alfred 51, 89
Lyttelton, Hon C.G. 40

MacDonald, Sir J.A. 69
Maidstone CC 25, 27
Maidstone Journal newspaper 12, 13, 14
Maidstone, Kent 12, 13, 14, 31, 50, 88, 89, 92, 93
Manchester Broughton CC 20, 88
Manet, Edouard 47
Marlborough , Wiltshire 88
Married v Single (1871) 86-87
Marsden, Thomas 35, 36
Marshall, George 42
Marsham, C.J.B. 47
Martin, E.W. 61
Martingell, William 15
Marden, Kent 14
Matfield, Kent 14
MCC 34, 35, 37, 38, 43, 44, 45, 47, 87, 93
Meade, Spencer 77, 78
Melbourne (Vic), Australia 21, 40
Melton Mowbray, Leicestershire 28
Merchant's Hotel, Philadelphia 73, **74**
Merion CC, Philadelphia 75
Milner family (Aylesford) 13
Milner Street, Chelsea 89
Mitre Hotel, Maidstone 31
Montreal, Canada 58, 68, 69, 70, 80
Montreal, Garrison Ground **54**, 70
Montreal Gazette newspaper 56, 57
Mortlock, William **50**
Mote Park, Maidstone 12, 27, 87

107

Index

Muralitharan, Muttiah 40
Mynn, Alfred 10, 13, 15, 24, 27, 32, 35
Mynn, W.P. 10

Newark, Nottinghamshire 28
New Cross, Kent 92
Newhall, C.A. 71, 75, 77, 78, 79, 81
Newhall, D.S. 75, 81
Newhall, G.M. 75, 76, 81
Newhall, R.S. 75
New Kent CC 13
Newmarket, Suffolk 50
Niagara Falls **54**, 69
New York 58, 59, 60, 61, 63, 64, 69, 70, 72, 74, 75, 80, 83
New York CC 62, 64
New York Times newspaper 62, 67
New York XXII cricket team 64, 66, 77, 80, 82
Nicetown Ground, Philadelphia **73**, 76, 82
Norley, Frederick 64, 65, 66, 71
North XI 26, 50, 55, 84, 85, 89
North American Gazette newspaper 75, 78
Nottingham 24, 35, 75
Nottinghamshire CCC 15, 18, 21, 24, 29, 56, 57, 91
Nyren, John 34

Old Stagers 33
Oval Cricket Ground, Kennington 16, 34, 39-40, 43, 49, 50, 51, 78
Oxford University CC 26, 91

Parr, George 24, 25, **32**, 51, 53, 84
Parr's XI, George (1859) 56
Patterson, W.S. 88
Pearson, Job 79, 80, 81
Philadelphia Athletic Club 82
Philadelphia XXII cricket team 56, 79, 80, 81, 82
Philadelphia CC 64, 71, 75, 77, 79, 80
Philadelphia, Pennsylvania 56, 58, 59, 71, 72, 74, 75, 80, 82
Pilch, Fuller 11, 15, 24
Players XI 26, 28, 32, 43, 91, 98
Players of South XI 53
Pooley, E.W. **50**, **57**, 58, 65, 72, 77, 79, 88, 98
Preston Hall, Aylesford 13
Prince, George and James 89, 91
Prince's Ground, Chelsea 89, **90**, 91, 92, 93
Prowse, W.J. 15
Pullin, A.W. ('Old Ebor') 48, 55
Pycroft, James 47

Queen's Head Inn, Southwark 31, 86
Queenstown (Cobh), Co Cork 59, 60

Rait Kerr, R.S. 47
Reading, Berkshire 27
Rogerson, W. 66
Rolvenden, Kent 7, 8, 11, 13, 31

Rowbotham, Joseph **57**, 58, 60, 66, 67, 70, 72, 77
Rugby School 48, 88
Rye, Sussex 8

St George's CC, New York 55, 56, 58, 62, 63, 64, 65, 67, 68, 70, 71, 82
St Saviour's Church, Southwark 31
Sandgate Hill ground, Folkestone 46
Sewell, Thomas, sen **50**
Seymour, Horatio 74
Shackleton, Derek 20
Shaw, Alfred 21, **54**, 57, **57**, 60, 65, 66, 69, 76, 77, 80
Sheffield, Yorkshire 35, 64
Sissons, Ric 13
Sleaford, Lincolnshire 27
Smith, John (Cambridge) **54**, 57, **57**, 65, 71, 77, 78, 79, 81, 82
South XI 26, 50
Southerton, James 21, 56, 98
Southborough, Kent 13
Southgate, Middlesex 39, 51
South Hampshire Regiment 31
Southwark, Surrey 31, 86, 89, 92
South Wiltshire XVIII cricket team 27
Spofforth, F.R. 18
Sporting Gazette journal 49, 58, 84, 85, 86, 89, 91
Sporting Life newspaper 41, 42, 43
Stamford, (seventh) Earl of 29, 88
Stamford, Lincolnshire 28
Staplehurst, Kent 13, 14
Stephenson, H.H. **33**, 51
Stilebridge, Kent 14, 16, 25
Stiller, B.E. 61
Stourbridge, Worcestershire 29
Stowmarket, Suffolk 25
Street, George 42
Surrey 15
Surrey CCC 15-16, 18, 26, 28, 36, 39, 42, 43, 45, 49, 51, 56, 57, 58, 88
Sussex 7, 15
Sussex CCC 15, 21, 24, 25, 27, 28, 35, 56, 58, 91

Tarrant, G.F. 18, 19, 21, **32**, 56, **57**, 65, 72, 76, 77
Tenterden, Kent 8, 14
Thoms, R.A. 48
Times, The newspaper 33, 51
Tinley, R.C. 29, **32**
Town Malling CC 25
Trinity College, Cambridge 29

Union Baseball Club, New York 68, 82, **83**
United England Eleven (UEE) 25, 26, 28, 29, 36, 39, 45, 46, 49, 50, 51
United North of England Eleven (UNEE) 51, 98
United South of England Eleven (USEE) 49, 50, **50**, 98
United States 53, 62, 69, 74
United States cricket team 58, 64, 79
Upper Fant Road, Maidstone **11**, 88

Index

Uppingham School 88

Walker, Thomas 34
Walker, V.E. 39, 40, 42, 55
Waterman, Augustus 77
Wenman, E.G. 10-11, 15, 32
West Kent CC 14
West Kent Wanderers CC 93
West Malling, Kent 12
West Wickham, Kent 28
White, F.S. 76
White Hart Inn, Chatham 14
Willes, John 34, 35
Willow CC, New York 64
Wills, T.W. 48

Willsher, Alice (daughter) 88, 97
Willsher (née Winser), Charlotte (mother) 7, 8
Willsher, Charlotte jun (sister) 12

Willsher, Edgar
  benefit matches 86-87
  best first-class bowling return 33
  birth 7-8
  Boston match 71-72
  bowling style 18-23
  bowls under-arm 39
  business fails 93
  captain of North American tour 54, 55, **57**
  childhood/education 10
  clashes within the CFFS committee 84
  club cricket 13-14
  coaching jobs 88
  debate over his action 32-38
  dies of liver cancer 94
  Enville Hall professional 29, 30, **30**, 31
  first-class debut 16, **16**
  first game after no-ball incident 45
  first season with AEE 27
  formation of new Kent club 32
  funeral 95
  gravestone 95, **96**
  hat-trick 53
  highest first-class score 46
  involvement in North-South schism 50
  journey across Atlantic 59-60
  last match as player 94
  leading first-class wicket-taker 28
  manager of English Eleven 51
  marriage 31
  Montreal match 69-70
  moves to Goudhurst and Maidstone 12
  New York matches 62-63, 64-67
  no-ball incident 39-44, **41**
  over-arm legalised 47
  Oxford University professional 26
  Philadelphian matches 75-81
  playing debut 12
  plays for UEE 25
  Prince's Ground professional 89-91
  probate granted 97
  secretary of USEE 49
  selected for aborted trip to Australia 85
  sets up as cricket outfitter 92
  single-wicket cricket 14
  umpiring 93-94

Willsher, Edgar jun (son) 88, 97
Willsher, Edith (daughter) 88, 97
Willsher, Ernest (son) 33, 88, 97
Willsher, George (brother) 10
Willsher, John (father) 7, 8
Willsher, John Edgar (son) 31, 53
Willsher, Robert (cousin) 31
Willsher (née Johnston), Sarah (wife) 31, 88
Willsher, Stephen (grandfather) 7, 8
Willsher, William 10, 12, 13, 88

Wisden, John 21, 24, 25, 27, 29, 36, 50, 53, 56
Wisden Cricketers' Almanack 25, 49, 51, 52, 87, 89, 94
Wister family (Philadelphia) 74, 75
Wootton, George 56
Worcestershire cricket team 29
Wright, George 64, 72
Wright, Samuel **64**, 65
Wright, W.H. 64, **64**, 65, 67, 72

Yardley, William 87
Yorkshire CCC 21, 56, 58, 94
Young America CC, Philadelphia 56, 63, 75, 79